# Stories
## to help you
# pray

Text copyright © Susan Lacy 2002
Illustrations copyright © Andy Robb 2002

The author asserts the moral right
to be identified as the author of this work

**Published by**
**The Bible Reading Fellowship**
First Floor, Elsfield Hall
15–17 Elsfield Way, Oxford OX2 8FG
ISBN 1 84101 188 6

First published 2002
10 9 8 7 6 5 4 3 2 1 0
All rights reserved

**Acknowledgments**
Unless otherwise stated, scripture quotations are quoted from the Good News Bible
published by The Bible Societies/HarperCollins Publishers Ltd, UK © American Bible
Society 1966, 1971, 1976, 1992, used with permission.

Scripture quotations taken from the *Holy Bible, New International Version*, copyright
© 1973, 1978, 1984 by International Bible Society. Used by permission of Hodder
& Stoughton Limited. All rights reserved. 'NIV' is a registered trademark of
International Bible Society. UK trademark 1448790.

A catalogue record for this book is available from the British Library

Printed and bound in Great Britain by
Bookmarque, Croydon

# Stories
## to help you
# pray

# Susan Lacy

**10 stories with guided prayer journeys for children**

*This book is dedicated to the memory of Mo Jowett,
who was a constant source of encouragement.*


*With thanks to Veronica Heley for her
generosity and help.
Special thanks also to Mrs Breton at St Peter's
School, Rawdon, and Mrs Hickman at Pool
Church of England school and their classes,
who helped to trial the stories.*

# Contents

# Introduction

## Notes for teachers

The stories and guided meditations in this book call upon children to use active imagination to journey into a Gospel scene, where they are able to meet Jesus. This is a way of teaching children how to pray in a form that will lead them into a lasting habit of meaningful prayer.

People have meditated on the Bible since Christianity began. They listened to the scriptures being read and committed portions of them to heart. They meditated on the Bible stories depicted in the beauty of stained glass. They read the scriptures slowly and meditatively, listening until a phrase or word attracted them and then holding it in their mind and heart. As the meaning of the words sank deep into the consciousness, so they were open to the transforming work of the Spirit within them, leading them to a living relationship with God.

In the 16th century, Ignatius of Loyola set down in his *Spiritual Exercises* a way of reflecting and meditating on the scriptures, using imagination to enter a Gospel scene. Through using the imagination in this way, Ignatius said, those who pray should come to know and experience the reality of Jesus in their lives. These meditations have now re-emerged and are being used by Christians of all denominations to engage their imaginations and encounter Christ in the depths of their hearts.

Through telling stories about Jesus, or telling the stories that Jesus told, we help children to build up a relationship with him. But our main purpose should be to help them to build that relationship with Jesus as he is present with us now, in the Spirit. Through meditating on the stories of Jesus, through using their creative imaginations to enter the world of the story and become part of it, through experiencing the Gospel stories in this way, children come to know God, the God who is present and active in his world now.

Meditation brings children to know the love of God. It also enables that love to express itself in their lives. As children meditate, they become calmer, more peaceful and loving, better able to concentrate and to exercise self-control. The Holy Spirit is working deep within them to enable them to grow up into the likeness of Jesus and learn to know the fullness of his presence in the centre of their hearts.

## Praying and meditating with a group or class

1. Decide which story you are going to read. The stories do not have to be read in order. Spend some time reflecting on the meditation first, in order to become comfortable with this form of prayer.

2. From the *Look out* section of the story, choose an activity to use after the meditation. You may need to prepare or collect materials first. Explain the activity to the group or class before you begin the story, so that the calmness after the prayer journey into it is not disrupted. If time is short, or if you prefer, you may wish to use the story and meditation alone.

3. It is recommended that each child use a special notebook to record his or her experiences during meditation. This notebook will be their prayer journal, used to record and reflect on their individual responses to their prayer journey. Over a period of time, they will have a continuing record of a deepening friendship with God.

Teachers may find, however, that posing directed questions helps some children to reflect on their experiences more fully. At the end of each meditation there are several questions for teachers to use (or they may devise their own), which will enable children to respond successfully in their journals. Make a copy of these questions for each child, and allow sufficient quiet, prayerful time for their responses. Assure children that prayer journals are private and will not be collected in. However, you may wish to have a sharing time, when children who wish to do so are invited to share their reflections and experiences with others.

4. It is important that the area in which the story and meditation are to take place is quiet, and that a peaceful, prayerful atmosphere has been established. A Bible, cross, candle or flowers can be placed as a centrepiece on a small table. Background music can be played to set the mood for the meditation. Soft instrumental music could be playing as the children come quietly together.

5. Children may sit in chairs or on the floor, but they must each have their own space, so that they do not distract one another.

6. When you are ready, read the story to the children. Ask them to listen to what God is saying through the story.

7. Before you begin the meditation, you may find it useful to teach the children how to relax. It helps if they can learn to sit in a comfortable position with a straight back and their head up. They can sit on a chair with both feet flat on the floor and their hands on their knees, or on the floor with their legs crossed and their hands on their thighs.

   Then ask them to close their eyes for a moment or two and just relax. They can tense each part of the body and then let go, if that is helpful—tense and let go the feet and legs, the arms and hands; tense and let go the stomach muscles, the shoulders; tense and let go the face. Finally, ask them to take one or two deep breaths and sit still and quietly.

8. Lead the children into the meditation. Ask them to look into the story with their imaginations in the way suggested in the *Look in* section. Lead them slowly and quietly on their prayer journey back through the story, pausing for a short while where indicated, allowing sufficient time for the imagery to take place, prompting their imaginations gently as they sit in the silence.

The more children know about the historical and social background of the story—how people lived and worked, what they ate, what they wore—the richer the picture in their imaginations will be. Use biblical commentaries, study guides, illustrations, photographs and so on, as preparation before you begin, to help the story come alive.

9. After the prayer journey, ask the children to 'look out' of the story and take its meaning with them into whatever activity they are going to do next, and into the rest of the day.

# Jesus
# the healer

A man with leprosy came to him and begged him on his knees, 'If you are willing, you can make me clean.'

**Mark 1:40–45**

**Key verse: 40 (NIV)**

# Introduction

We are all different from each other. No two people are the same. But we are all special to God. We are all equally important because we are his. Jesus reaches out to everyone to love and to heal, much to Rachel's amazement.

## Story

Rachel fled down the street that led to the busy marketplace, holding fast to her brother with one hand and her basket with the other. In an open doorway she stopped to catch her breath and glanced back the way they had come.

Then, telling her brother he must run faster, she dragged him behind her along the broad path that swept down the hillside and out of the village. Halfway down the hill, her brother let go of her hand, flung himself on the springy grass with a sob and began to cry.

'It's all right, Gideon,' Rachel told him, flinging herself down next to him.

Squinting round, she stared back up the hill. 'They're not following us now. They'd never dare chase us all the way.'

With a sharp intake of breath, Rachel dabbed the red gashes that the stones had made on her arm, gently with the edge of her mantle. 'Leper, leper,' the boys had shouted as they threw the stones. 'Unclean, unclean,' they yelled as they chased Rachel and her brother through the narrow alleyways and winding streets.

Rachel hated them, especially Aaron, the ringleader, the boy who had made their lives a misery ever since their father had been told he had leprosy and had been sent away. Leprosy was a terrible skin disease and it could not be cured, Rachel knew.

Lepers were feared and despised because people thought that if a leper touched them, they might get leprosy too. Banned, shunned and dreaded, they were driven away from their homes to live alone or with other lepers.

'I want to go home,' Gideon began to wail.

'Well you can't,' snapped Rachel. 'Mother's not feeling well today and someone's got to take father some food.'

Pulling her brother to his feet, she picked up the basket and trudged off ahead of him towards the shore of Lake Galilee, where a maze of caves made a home for the banished lepers. Abruptly, the hillside dipped beside a fist of grey boulders clinging to the earth. Here Rachel stopped and glanced around. She opened the basket and took out the bread and the fish that her mother had wrapped carefully in a cloth.

Then, taking a deep breath, she called out, 'Father! Father, are you there? It's me, Rachel.'

Ahead of her, a small shower of stones went hurtling down the hillside. Then a hand appeared from behind the rocks and began to wave. Cautiously, Rachel descended, reached a broad stone slab that jutted like a table from the earth, and left the package on it.

She began to climb back up the hill, but something made her pause and turn. Down below stood her father, his clothes filthy and torn, his face a mass of ulcers and sores, staring longingly after her. 'Father,' she gasped in a mixture of pity and horror, and turning her back on him, her eyes blinded by tears, she stumbled slowly to the top of the hill.

There was no sign of Aaron and the other boys as they made their way back home to the small stone house set high on the hillside. As they approached, a buzz of voices greeted them from the open doorway.

'Rachel, Gideon,' their mother called excitedly as they stepped inside. 'Your Aunt Joanna has been telling me about a healer called Jesus.'

Rachel greeted the bulky figure of her aunt sitting comfortably on the floor. Aunt Joanna was her father's sister, and one of the few people who still came to visit them, now that her father had leprosy. Rachel sat down next to her.

'He's a teacher and he's been going all over Galilee telling people about God,' explained her aunt. 'He's coming to the village tomorrow to preach in the synagogue. And he can heal people, just by laying his hands on them.' She paused and leaned forward. 'I'm sure he can heal your father, too.'

'How can he heal him, Aunt Joanna?' asked Rachel. 'No one can heal leprosy.'

'He healed my cousin Sara of a fever,' said her aunt in a firm voice. 'There she was in bed and her daughter's husband Simon brought Jesus in to see her. And he went to her, took her hand and helped her up. The fever left her, just like that, and she began to make a meal for them.'

'But no one would touch a leper,' insisted Rachel.

'Trust in God and don't be afraid. That's what your father always used to say,' her aunt reminded her. 'You must go and tell him tomorrow, Rachel. Tell him to hide outside the village until he sees a tall man with a great crowd following him. Tell him that Jesus can heal him.'

The sun rose pale and golden above the dark hills next morning. With an urgent shake of her shoulder, Rachel's mother woke her. After a hurried breakfast of bread and milk, she set off down the winding streets, leaving Gideon still sleeping. Her mother had wanted her to take him too, but Rachel had insisted it would be quicker without him.

The narrow streets were deserted, except for an occasional woman, water-jug held high on her head, making her way from the well. Sparrows fluttered in the olive trees as Rachel ran, then walked, down the hill. Goats bleated in the distance, but Rachel hardly heard them for the echo of her father's words ringing in her ears. 'Trust in God, and don't be afraid.'

But where was God now? she wondered. Her father had trusted in God all his life, but he had still caught leprosy. Rachel felt completely alone as she found herself standing beside the grey boulders once more, questions spinning round inside her head.

'Father,' she called, into the empty blue sky. And again, 'Father.'

No reply, nothing. She began to work cautiously over the dirt and rocks until she reached the stone table. Suddenly she remembered: her father only came to the meeting place on certain days.

Taking a deep breath, her heart pounding like a hammer inside her chest, Rachel slipped and stumbled down a rough pathway, until she reached a rocky shelf where she could stand and rest. Below her, a honeycomb of caves led down to the lake: they were dark sockets where the eyes of the lepers looked out on to a hostile world.

Rachel stared. Figures were moving in and out of the darkness— some hideous and misshapen, some hobbling without feet or toes. Clenching her fists by her sides in an effort to stop herself from fleeing back up the hill, Rachel began to call her father's name.

'Jacob!' she yelled. 'Jacob, it's your daughter, Rachel!'

Again and again she called until, at last, a figure emerged from the shadows and began to shuffle towards her. He stopped under the rock where she was standing, and shaded his eyes with his hand.

'Father,' she said urgently, 'you must come up to the village. There's a healer—Jesus, his name is—and he's preaching at the synagogue today.' She hesitated, her voice shaking, before she went on. 'Aunt Joanna says he can heal lepers. She says you must hide until you see a tall man with a crowd following him.'

Rachel stopped. Other lepers had emerged from the caves now. She turned away from her father in fear and panic. Scrambling back up the hillside, she glanced behind her once to see her father slowly and painfully following.

At the edge of the village market square, Rachel froze. Aaron was standing next to a stall selling fruit, and as she pulled her mantle over her head and tried to hide, she heard his voice cry, 'Leper! Unclean, unclean!'

Rachel glanced around quickly, hoisted her tunic to her knees and made for the nearest alleyway. Without looking back, she raced up the rough stone path, shutting her ears to the cries of 'Leper! Dirty leper!' as Aaron pounded up the alley behind her.

At the top of the hill, the path branched into two. Stopping for a second to catch her breath, Rachel ignored the one that climbed to the slopes beyond the village and set off, stumbling and skidding, down the other. At the bottom of the hill, her side aching and her heart beating uncontrollably, Rachel slid to a halt.

'Leper,' Aaron panted as he ran up behind her. 'Dirty, stinking leper,' he said, bending down. He was picking up stones.

'Leave me alone!' Rachel shouted. She covered her face with her arm as the stones came stinging towards her. 'It's not my fault my father's got leprosy.'

'No, but it's his fault, isn't it?' Aaron sneered. 'He must've done something really bad, your father, to get leprosy. Everyone knows God punishes you if you do something bad.'

'That's not true. My father's a good man,' said Rachel. 'But you, you're just a coward.'

Aaron dropped the stones he had ready to throw. 'A coward? I'm not afraid of anything,' he snarled.

'Prove it, then,' said Rachel. 'Come and see my father.' She beckoned him to follow her. 'That's if you're not too scared.'

A crowd was trailing the tall figure walking towards them as Rachel, with Aaron trudging reluctantly behind her, reached the village wall. 'This must be the man called Jesus they're all talking about,' she began to tell him. 'They say he can...'

All at once, a man slunk out from the shadows. He stumbled forward, hesitated, stared longingly in the direction of Jesus.

'Father!' Rachel cried.

'Leper!' shrieked Aaron, shrinking away from her as her father hobbled forward.

On the edge of the crowd, screams rang out and Aaron's cry of 'Leper!' was echoed in open, frightened mouths. Like a flock of scared sheep, the people scattered as Rachel's father came towards them. Then, to Rachel's astonishment, although some men were trying to hold him back, Jesus walked forward to meet him.

Instantly, the leper stopped, swaying on his feet, and fell on his swollen knees in the dust. Lifting his shrivelled hands, he raised his ravaged face and pleaded, 'If you want to, you can make me well again.'

Jesus said nothing, but let his eyes wander searchingly over the leper's ulcers and sores. Aaron drew nearer as Rachel watched, until they were both standing together, hardly daring to breathe. Suddenly, Jesus smiled. Then, to Rachel's amazement, he stretched out his hand and laid it, gently, on her father's head.

'I want to heal you,' he said. 'You're well again.'

Very lightly, Jesus passed his hands over the leprous skin. Rachel shuddered. She didn't know how he could bear to do it. But at Jesus' touch, the sores and ulcers seemed to melt away, leaving her father's skin smooth and healthy. Full of joy, he gazed up at Jesus, looking into his face, studying every feature, as though he never wanted to forget one detail of the face of the man who had healed him.

Taking his hands in his, Jesus helped Rachel's father gently to his feet and said in a stern voice, 'Go to the priest now, and show him that you are healed. But don't stop to tell anyone how you were cured.'

By now, the crowd had begun to gather again. Jesus let the clean hands fall, nodded briefly and swung round to walk towards them.

Tears of joy running down their cheeks, Rachel and her father smiled at each other. 'Trust in God, and don't be afraid,' her father said.

'I was afraid,' muttered Aaron, staring past them. 'But Jesus wasn't. I'm sorry, Rachel. For everything. God doesn't punish us, does he? He loves us.'

'And I didn't trust,' said Rachel. 'But I do now. Now I *know* where God is.'

## Look in

In a moment, you are going to close your eyes and imagine the world of the story as if you were there. Become part of it. You can be yourself or Rachel, or anyone in the story you want to be. Picture yourself there, then move through the story in your imagination as the person you have chosen to be. Or, if you prefer, you can imagine you are trying to describe what is happening to someone else.

✤

Now, close your eyes, sit up straight and put your hands on your knees. Keep your body still, as this helps your mind to be still and concentrate as you go on your prayer journey. Take a deep breath and relax. Sit still and quiet and spend a few moments being with God, saying slowly and silently in your mind, '*Be still and know that I am God.*'

✤

Picture Rachel and her brother running out of the village and down the hillside. Watch Gideon as he flings himself on the grass and begins to cry. See Rachel fling herself down next to him... Look at Rachel as she dabs the cuts on her arm. Think about how she is feeling...

Now follow the children as they trudge off towards the caves where the lepers live. Watch as Rachel takes out the food, calls to her father and climbs down to the stone table... See Rachel turn and look at her father. See her father look at her. Wonder what they are thinking...

Picture the children returning home. Listen to their Aunt Joanna talking about Jesus. Think about how she is feeling...

Imagine Rachel running down the hill next morning. Watch as she makes her way to the caves... Look at her standing alone beside the grey boulders. Hear the echo of her father's words, 'Trust in God, and don't be afraid.' Think how she is feeling...

Now, follow her down the rocky path. Imagine the dark caves and the lepers moving in and out of them... Hear her call her father's name. Watch her father shuffle towards her and listen to what she says. Wonder what he is thinking...

See Rachel racing up the alleyway with Aaron pounding behind her. Hear him shout 'Leper! Dirty leper!' Follow them as they stumble to the bottom of the hill and stop... Look at Aaron as he picks up the stones. Watch Rachel as she covers her face with her arm. Hear them as they shout at each other. Listen to Aaron say, 'God punishes you if you do something bad.' ...

Picture them as they walk towards Jesus. See Rachel's father slink out from the shadows. Hear the crowd scream, 'Leper!' and watch them scatter... Look at Jesus as he meets the leper. See the leper fall to his knees. Hear him say, 'If you want to, you can make me well again.' ...

Picture Jesus touching the leper. Watch the sores and ulcers melt away. See the joy on the leper's face. Think how he is feeling... Listen to Aaron and Rachel as Jesus walks away. Think how he has made them feel.

Now sit in the silence for a few moments more and think about what God is saying to you through the story. Think about how you feel. Think about what you would like to say to God and to Jesus. Thank God for his love.

## Questions for reflection

- Who were you in the prayer journey through the story?
- What did you think about the things Aaron and the other boys had done to Rachel and her brother at the beginning of the story?
- How did you feel when you saw Rachel and her father looking at each other after she had left him the food?
- What did you think when you heard Aunt Joanna talking about Jesus?
- Describe how you felt when you saw the caves and the lepers.
- How did you feel when you saw Aaron chasing Rachel?
- What did you think when you heard Aaron say, 'God punishes you if you do something bad'?
- What did you think when you heard Aaron and Rachel talking at the end of your prayer journey?
- What was it like to see Jesus heal Rachel's father?
- What do you think Jesus is saying to you now? What do you want to say to him?

1. Use your prayer journal. Write down what you saw, heard, felt and did during your prayer journey. Use the *Questions for reflection* to help you if you want.

2. Read the story in your Bible. Read it slowly and carefully. Read it more than once. Listen to the words, and if a word or sentence draws your attention, hold it in your mind. Think over it silently—dwell on it until it sinks deep into your heart. Carry it with you into whatever you are doing for the rest of the day.

3. Write about a time when you felt lonely, rejected or unhappy.

4. Look at the face of the person sitting next to you. Describe it in detail, either through drawing, painting or writing.

5. Choose an object from nature, such as a stone, shell, piece of wood or pine cone. Close your eyes and feel the object. Is it rough or smooth, hard or soft, heavy or light? Now open your eyes. Look at the colour, the shape, the patterns. Write down anything it makes you feel or think of.

**Prayer**

Dear God, thank you that we are all different. Thank you that we are all special. Help us to treat others as we want to be treated, accepting them as you accept and love us. Amen

# The hole in the roof

A few days later Jesus went back to Capernaum, and the news spread that he was at home. So many people came together that there was no room left, not even out in front of the door. Jesus was preaching the message to them when four men arrived, carrying a paralysed man to Jesus. Because of the crowd, however, they could not get the man to him. So they made a hole in the roof right above the place where Jesus was.

**Mark 2:1–12**

 **Key verses: 1–4a**

22

# Introduction

In The Lord's Prayer, Jesus taught us to pray, 'Forgive us our sins, as we forgive those who sin against us.' To forgive others is not an easy thing to do. To forgive is to let go of hatred and anger, to let go of the desire to hurt as we have been hurt. To be forgiven is a wonderful thing. It is freeing and healing and allows us to grow and to change. Simon experienced this when he heard Jesus say, 'Everything you have done wrong is forgiven.'

# Story

'Stop, thief, stop him!' bellowed the great bull of a man who charged, cloak flapping, from behind the fruit stall. Shaking a hairy fist, he pounded through the dry dust of the Capernaum marketplace, chasing a small boy now dodging barefoot through the gathering crowd.

'Hey, you boy!' 'Stop!' 'Catch him!' People called to each other as he scuttled between them.

Disappearing deeper and deeper into the dense throng, the boy thrust the two oranges he was clutching down inside the front of his tunic . Now that he could no longer hear the bellows of the angry stallholder, he laughed to himself as he thought how the mountain of oranges had collapsed when he had taken two from the bottom. Face purple with rage, the stallholder had danced desperately up and down, trying to catch the oranges with one hand and him with the other.

Serve him right, great ugly lump, thought the boy. What did he know about being poor and hungry? About having nothing to eat all day but the dry scraps the women threw out for the dogs?

The boy felt sure that the stallholder would not catch him now, so he allowed himself to be swept along by the swelling crowd into the courtyard of a neat whitewashed house. The wooden door stood open, but the house must be packed with people, the boy decided, looking around, for no one was able to move in or out.

Yet men and women swarmed around the house like ants, trying to find a way inside. They stood on tiptoe, straining to see over the shoulders of those in front. They pressed against each other, desperately trying to push their way to the door.

'Why is everyone trying to get into that house?' the boy asked a man who was attempting to squeeze past him.

The man stared at him with eyes as round as the oranges hidden in the boy's tunic. 'Are you stupid?' he gasped. 'Don't you know anything? There's Jesus in there, Jesus of Nazareth. They say he cured a leper. Imagine that—a leper. And scores of other people, too. Everyone wants to see him.' With that, the man slipped sideways past the boy and vanished into a web of arms and legs.

'If everyone's so bothered about seeing Jesus,' the boy muttered to himself, 'they're not going to bother about finding me.'

He turned his back on the crowd and began to elbow his way through the people until he reached the wooden steps at the side of the house. He scrambled up to the flat roof and turned to perch at the top, so that he could watch what happened.

The crowd seemed to be swaying like grass in the wind as he stared over their heads. In the distance he saw four men, hurrying down the street towards the house, carrying another man between them on a stretcher. The boy's eyes followed the men as they reached the edge of the courtyard, stopped and tried to force their way through. But no one would move so much as a step to let them pass.

Then one of the men pointed to the flat roof. The others nodded, and carefully they picked up the stretcher and made their way to the side of the house.

One of them looked up the steps at the boy and called out, 'Hey, you, what's your name?'

The boy hesitated for a moment, then, 'Simon!' he called back.

'Well, Simon, stop perching up there like a sparrow in a sycamore tree, and come down and give us a hand.'

Simon slid down the steps backwards and landed at the foot of the stretcher. He stared curiously at the man lying on it, whose paralysed legs were as twisted and knotted as a vine. What did the man's friends intend to do? he wondered. By the look of him he must have been paralysed for years. He was thin and bent, and his body was covered in sores.

'Enough of that gawping, Simon,' said the man who had called him down. 'We need your help to get the stretcher up on the roof.'

'On the roof?' asked Simon.

'Yes, the roof. We're going to dig a hole in it and let our friend down directly to Jesus. We'll never get him anywhere near Jesus otherwise. Now, you steady the steps while we heave him up.'

Simon held on to the steps as the four men hoisted the stretcher on to their shoulders and began to push and pull it up to the roof. At the top they placed the paralysed man in a shady spot and, as Simon scrambled up after them, they started to dig. Because the roof was flat and made of clay, in no time at all they had dug out the filling between two of the beams and opened a long hole.

Simon shook his head in wonder as he watched them. 'Jesus must be someone special for you to do all this.'

'He is,' one of them replied, wiping the sweat from his forehead with the back of his hand. 'They say Jesus of Nazareth can heal anyone who comes to him.'

Now the four men tied ropes to the ends of the stretcher. Next they carried it to the edge of the hole. Together they leaned forward and gently lowered their paralysed friend into the room below. When the stretcher touched the floor, the men dropped the ropes and peered anxiously through the hole to see what would happen.

Simon peered through the hole too. The stretcher had come to rest just in front of a tall man standing as still and straight as a cypress tree, in the middle of a mass of people. This man must be Jesus, thought Simon.

Faces gaped back from the space below. Pieces of clay and wood were everywhere. People had pushed backwards, making way for the stretcher, and now Jesus looked up too.

His steady gaze was full of understanding as his eyes met the expectant faces peering down at him. He looked from them to the sick man and back to them again. Then Jesus smiled and his whole face shone as if a light had been lit in the stuffy darkness of the crowded room. Simon gasped. Jesus seemed to be looking directly at him now with a look that said 'Yes, I can help anyone, if they trust in me.'

Then Jesus gazed down at the sick man again and the watching crowd grew quiet. In a calm voice he said gently, 'Don't worry, my son. Everything you have done wrong is forgiven.'

The four men on the roof stared at each other in surprise.

Why did Jesus say that? they wondered. They had expected him to heal their friend straight away, that was why they had brought him. The people below were surprised as well.

Immediately after Jesus had spoken, some of the priests and teachers in the crowd began to mutter among themselves. Soon they were muttering loudly enough for everyone to hear.

'Who does Jesus think he is?' they declared. 'Only God can forgive people.'

At once Jesus turned on them as if they were rats in a corner. 'Why are you thinking such things?' he challenged in a voice like steel. The priests and teachers cowered away and continued muttering among themselves.

But Simon did not listen to what they said next. All he could think of were Jesus' words, 'Everything you have done wrong is forgiven.' Over and over in his mind he chanted them. 'Everything you have done wrong is forgiven.' And it seemed to Simon that Jesus had been speaking to him too.

He slipped his hand inside the front of his tunic and felt the two oranges he had stolen, still nestling there. He thought of all the other things he had stolen in the past—not just when he had been hungry, but when he had been bored or angry or jealous that someone else had more than him—and his face burned red with shame. But Jesus had said, 'Everything you have done wrong is forgiven.'

Just then, Jesus' voice grew louder. 'Which is it easier to say to a man like this, "Everything you have done wrong is forgiven", or "Get up and walk"?' he asked the priests and the teachers. 'I will show you that I have the power to forgive.'

Simon peered down at him again and saw that he had bent over the man on the stretcher. In a calm, even voice, Jesus said, 'Get up. Lift up your bed and go home.'

At once the crowd was hushed. Silence muffled the whole room like fog on a winter's day. Everyone stared at the paralysed man, the man who had not been able to move for years.

Slowly, the man rolled over. He sat up and pulled himself, trembling, to his feet. Then he picked up his stretcher, thanked

Jesus and walked out of the room as the stunned crowd made way for him.

In an instant, his four friends had scrambled down from the roof, whooping and calling in praise and astonishment. Simon stood up and stared after them, amazed, as if he was in a dream, until shouts from the courtyard below brought him suddenly to his senses.

'You up there. Yes, you boy. I want a word with you.'

It was the man from the fruit stall, waving his hairy arms in the air and looking fiercer than ever. Simon's heart began to race. He glanced round frantically, searching for a way to escape. It was then that Jesus' words echoed again in his head. 'Everything you have done wrong is forgiven.'

Simon stood at the top of the steps. He thought of Jesus' face smiling up at him and the look that said "Yes, I can help anyone, if they trust in me.' Taking a deep breath, he clambered down and walked across the courtyard. From inside his tunic he pulled out the oranges and held them in front of him.

'Your... your oranges... Here... I'm... I'm sorry,' he stammered as he reached the man.

The stallholder towered over him and raised one hand in the air. Simon covered his face with his arm and waited for the hand to strike. But it never did.

Instead, to Simon's amazement, the man put his arm around him and shook his head. 'Keep the oranges,' he muttered. 'You look as if you need them more than me, lad. I was searching for you in the crowd. Then people told me how Jesus healed the man on the stretcher. They told me what he said.' He coughed loudly and swallowed hard. 'I've done things that need forgiving, too.'

Together they walked out of the courtyard, the man and the boy. In the distance, they could still see the once-paralysed man and his friends waving their arms in joy. And behind them, still muttering bitterly to each other, a small group of angry men slunk silently away.

In a moment, you are going to close your eyes and imagine the world of the story as if you were there. Become part of it. You can be yourself or Simon, or anyone in the story you want to be. Picture yourself there, then move through the story in your imagination as the person you have chosen to be. Or, if you prefer, you can imagine you are trying to describe what is happening to someone else.

✤

Now, close your eyes, sit up straight and put your hands on your knees. Keep your body still, as this helps your mind to be still and concentrate as you go on your prayer journey. Take a deep breath and relax. Sit still and quiet and spend a few moments being with God, saying slowly and silently in your mind, '*Be still and know that I am God.*'

✤

Now, imagine the market place in Capernaum. It's a hot day. The sun is high in the sky. Imagine the stalls, and the white, flat-roofed buildings... Picture the stallholder behind his stall, selling fruit...

Now watch the boy creep up on him and take the oranges. Watch the stallholder as he runs after him... See the boy disappear into the crowd. Listen to the people shouting...

Smell the sweat from their bodies as the people press forward into the courtyard of the house where Jesus is teaching... Now follow the boy as he climbs up on to the roof.

Look at the crowd below... Picture the four friends and the man on the stretcher. Look at their anxious faces. Watch them make their way to the bottom of the steps… Touch the stretcher. Help them to pick it up. Feel how heavy it is…

Help the friends to make a hole in the roof. Dig out the clay and pull up the wood… Look through the hole into the room below. Wonder what the people in the room are thinking…

Look at Jesus. Watch him look up, then down. Watch him look at Simon. Listen to what he says. 'Everything you have done wrong is forgiven.' … Now notice the priests and teachers. Look at their faces. Listen to what they are saying…

Watch Jesus as he heals the paralysed man. Watch the man get up, pick up his stretcher and walk away…

Picture Simon standing at the top of the steps. Picture the stallholder standing below. Watch Simon as he climbs down the steps and walks towards him… Listen to what they say to each other. See them walk away together…

See the priests and the teachers walk away too. Look at their faces. Think about how they are feeling.

❖

Now sit in the silence for a few moments more and think about what God is saying to you through the story. Think about how you feel. Think about what you would like to say to God and to Jesus. Thank God for his love.

## Questions for reflection

- Who were you in the prayer journey through the story?
- How did you feel when you saw the boy take the oranges?

- What did you think when you saw the men with their friend on the stretcher?
- What was it like, helping them make a hole in the roof?
- Describe how you felt when you looked at Jesus.
- What did you think when you heard Jesus say, 'Everything you have done wrong is forgiven'?
- How did you feel when you saw the paralysed man get up?
- How did you feel when you heard the stallholder talking to Simon?
- What do you think Jesus is saying to you? What do you want to say to him?

**Look out**

1. Use your prayer journal. Write down what you saw, heard, felt and did during your prayer journey. Use the *Questions for reflection* to help you if you want.

2. Read the story in your Bible. Read it slowly and carefully. Read it more than once. Listen to the words, and if a word or sentence draws your attention, hold it in your mind. Think over it silently—dwell on it until it sinks deep into your heart. Carry it with you into whatever you are doing for the rest of the day.

3. How do you feel when someone doesn't forgive you? Write a letter asking someone to forgive you for what you've done to them. Write a letter forgiving someone for what they've done to you.

4. Write a prayer to thank God for all the good things in your life.
5. Make a bookmark. On one side of a piece of card, write, 'Be still and know that I am God.' On the other side, write a poem or the prayer you have just written. Decorate your bookmark, and put a tassel in the end.

# Storm on
# the lake

On the evening of that same day Jesus said to his
disciples, 'Let us go across to the other side of the
lake.' So they left the crowd; the disciples got into
the boat in which Jesus was already sitting,
and they took him with them.

**Mark 4:35–41**

 **Key verses: 35–36a**

# Introduction

It's not always easy to trust in God, especially when we're afraid. But Jesus is always with us, ready to bring peace even in the middle of the wildest storm, as Isaac and Peter find out.

## Story

'Jesus is back!' the young woman's excited voice called from the hillside above the lake.

Isaac laid the fishing-net he was helping to mend out on the tufted grass. He shaded his eyes with his hand and squinted up to where the woman stood, waving impatiently.

The fishermen folding their nets in the boat by the rocks stowed them away in the stern and jumped heavy-footed on to the yellow sand. 'Did you hear that, Isaac?' one of them said, his gnarled face creased in joy. 'Jesus is back. And Peter and Andrew will be with him, and James and John. We're going to hear him teach. Are you coming, boy?'

Isaac shook his head and went on mending the tears in the net. 'Too much to do,' he mumbled.

'Please yourself,' the fisherman shrugged. He set off after the others who were scrambling over the rocky hillside to where the woman still stood.

Once they had all disappeared from view, Isaac thrust the net to one side and sat back against a cold slab of rock, thinking he would sit there until the sun fell and the blue water darkened and the fishermen came back.

'Jesus.' The name shot angrily from his lips as he hurled a stone as far as he could across the sand. Jesus had taken away his best friend, Peter—big, burly, kind-hearted Peter who had been like a father to him ever since his own father had died.

And now, instead of scudding over the lake in his boat, oars dipping and rising, nets ready to whirl into the deep water, Peter was wandering around the towns and villages of Galilee with Jesus. Instead of slippery, flapping fish, he was fishing for people.

'Fishing for people.' Isaac laughed out loud. Those were the words Jesus had used when he had called Peter and his brother Andrew, and their friends James and John, to follow him. 'Come, follow me,' Jesus said, 'and I will make you fishers of people.' And they'd left their boats, and their homes and families, and gone.

Fishing for people. What a stupid idea! What could be better than fishing for fish? Isaac wanted to know. To be out on a boat with Peter, the biggest, the bravest and the best fisherman in the whole of Galilee, was the most exciting thing in the world. But now Peter had gone, and nothing would ever be the same again.

Slowly, Isaac stood up. So Jesus was back, and Peter would be with him. Well, he didn't want to see them. Let the others go. He stared up at the blue sky and the wheeling birds, and thoughts began to gather like storm-clouds inside his head.

What if he did go and see them, after all? Told Jesus just what he thought of him and begged Peter to come back? Maybe, when Peter saw how much he missed him, he would leave that wandering storyteller and come home. Yes, that's just what he'd do, he decided.

Face set in a determined frown, he turned his back on the boats and began to climb up the hillside. Reaching the top, he followed a well-worn path down a slope starry with flowers, skirted a field further along the lake's edge and stopped when he saw the great crowd of people. This was the place where he would find Peter, he knew. Crowds followed Jesus as sure as summer followed spring.

Isaac pushed his way through the throng, passed fisher-men and farmers, mothers with small children, beggars and tax collectors. Pressing forward, they spilled on to the banks of the lake down to the water's edge, where a fishing-boat was moored a short distance from the shore. Sitting in the boat was Jesus, facing the people, telling stories and teaching in a powerful voice that resounded like a temple-gong over the still, blue water.

It rang in Isaac's ears as he searched anxiously for Peter. And then he saw him, holding back the press of people at one side almost single-handedly. Like a rock the big man stood firm, arms outstretched, muscle and bone taut against the bodies straining behind him who were threatening to jump into the water to get to Jesus.

After a while, when he seemed sure that the crowd had settled just to sitting or standing, Peter jumped into the shallows himself and let the water lap around his legs as he listened intently to Jesus.

'Peter!' Isaac called urgently from out of the crowd. And again, 'Peter!' as he stumbled over the tufted grass and squatting people towards him.

Peter turned his head. His brown eyes shone and his great laughing mouth opened like a cavern, now that he saw who was calling him.

'Isaac!' he boomed. 'Isaac, lad!' He waded to the water's edge and in an instant had hoisted himself on to the bank again and pulled Isaac to sit down next to him.

'Well, Isaac,' said Peter, his arm resting affectionately across Isaac's shoulders, 'I am glad to see you. Seems like years since I went away.'

'And I'm glad to see you,' said Isaac. 'I've missed you so much, Peter. Fishing's not the same without you.'

Peter grinned. 'We had some fun going out in that boat, didn't we? Do you remember the time you fell into a net full of wet fish?'

Isaac nodded. 'And do you remember the time when you fell overboard and came up with a catfish clinging to your beard?'

Peter squeezed Isaac's shoulder and roared with laughter, then stopped abruptly when some of the people around them began to complain that they could not hear Jesus.

'Why don't you come back, Peter?' Isaac asked the big man. 'You can't be happy wandering around after a storytelling teacher who's never caught a fish in his life.'

Peter gazed out across the water to where Jesus was sitting and suddenly his whole face flooded with love. 'He catches fish all right, Isaac,' he murmured. 'He caught me, and I thought I was the safest fish in the sea.' He gestured with his arm towards the people. 'And look at these. Hooked, every one.'

'But what for, Peter? What's the point?'

'There's something about him, Isaac. Something special.' Peter's voice grew soft now and his eyes shone. 'When he speaks, you know that he means what he says. He understands people. He loves them, no matter who they are or what they've done. He heals people.' Peter turned and smiled at Isaac's stubborn face. 'There's a power in him... a power I don't understand. It's almost like...' Peter groped for words. 'Almost like he was love itself.'

'Power... love,' spluttered Isaac angrily. 'You've gone soft in your head. You're the powerful one. The big fisherman, the best fisherman, the...'

'Stop!' ordered Peter. 'That's enough. You go back to catching your fish, and leave me to catch mine.' He turned away from Isaac and jumped into the water, wading out to where the other disciples were climbing now into Jesus' boat.

Evening had crept stealthily over the hillside and enveloped the people and the lake in a soft coverlet of grey. Men, women and children started their slow journey home. Boats scudded purposefully across the face of the water. Isaac stared after Peter, and the words his friend had spoken seemed to echo inside his head. 'There's a power in him… a power I don't understand… like he was love itself.' Then, on an impulse, Isaac jumped into the shallows too.

Waves washed around him thick and heavy as he waded out towards the boats. Men were shouting and hoisting sails, and in the half-light no one saw Isaac as he hauled himself into Jesus' boat. He crawled under a pile of oiled skins and lay listening to the sail flapping and the gentle creak of timber as men moved up and down.

Slipping out on to the open lake, the boat began to head for the far shore. Other boats followed and the convoy sped swiftly and smoothly through the water. Before long, Isaac had fallen asleep. But his sleep was soon broken by the flash of lightning and the crack of thunder and the deck pitching and rolling under his body.

A sudden storm had hurled itself across the lake, shattering the calm and flinging the boats against the mounting waves as if they were splinters of wood. Isaac scrambled to his feet from under the oiled skins and saw James and John clutching at the ropes, trying to drag the sail in though the wind was tearing it to shreds.

The boat pitched and tossed like a wild horse. Water broke over the bow and a wave slammed Isaac under. Blinded for a moment, he struggled to his feet again as lightning lit up the whole lake in a blaze. Isaac rubbed his eyes. In the stern, curled up and asleep on a small cushion, lay Jesus.

Sleeping, Isaac thought contemptuously. At a time like this. What use is that?

Wave after wave crashed around the boat until, suddenly, Peter leaped through them as if from nowhere. Seizing hold of the ropes with James and John, he hung on with his powerful hands, and threw his body backwards in a mighty effort to control the sail. Isaac fixed his gaze on Peter, his eyes wet with tears, his heart full of love as he watched the big fisherman wrestle with all his strength against the storm. Brave, fearless Peter. Now they would be saved.

Peter turned his head. He caught sight of Isaac and his eyes opened wide. Then he let go of the ropes, stumbled sideways, put out his hand to steady himself and shouted, 'Save us, Master, save us!' Isaac stared in disbelief as Peter scrambled towards Jesus. Peter was afraid.

Under the jagged flash of lightning, Isaac saw Jesus sit up. Peter was yelling now, his voice hoarse with anger and fear. 'Master, don't you care? We're going to die!'

Jesus stood up, steady as a rock. He turned his face to the wind and cried out 'Peace!' in a voice more powerful than the thunder itself. He spread his hands towards the water and cried, 'Be still!' Instantly, the wind dropped and the waves fell and a great calm settled on the water.

Isaac's ears echoed with the sudden silence. No one spoke. Peter cowered in the bottom of the boat. The others huddled in a shivering heap.

Slowly, Jesus turned to look at his terrified disciples and shook his head. 'Why are you so afraid?' he asked, his eyes full of sadness and love. 'Do you still have no trust in me?'

But Isaac was not afraid. His eyes shone with the wonder of the miracle he had just seen. Now he knew why Peter wanted to follow Jesus. He had felt the power that Peter could not understand. He had seen the love in Jesus' eyes.

Peter and the other disciples lifted their heads and stared at Jesus in amazement. 'Who is this man?' they whispered among themselves. 'Even the wind and the waves obey him.'

Isaac put his hand on Peter's arm and the two of them went to sit apart as the boat continued its journey. 'I'm sorry for everything I said, Peter,' said Isaac. 'Now I understand why you want to follow Jesus. There was a storm in my head like the storm on the lake. But Jesus has stilled that too.'

Peter shook his head. 'I'm the one who should be sorry. You showed me something about love and trust. You trusted me, but I didn't trust Jesus. I hope I never come to doubt him again.'

## Look in

In a moment, you are going to close your eyes and imagine the world of the story as if you were there. Become part of it. You can be yourself, Isaac or Peter, or anyone in the story you want to be. Picture yourself there, then move through the story in your imagination as the person you have chosen to be. Or, if you prefer, you can imagine you are trying to describe what is happening to someone else.

Now, close your eyes, sit up straight and put your hands on your knees. Keep your body still, as this helps your mind to be still and concentrate as you go on your prayer journey. Take a deep breath and relax. Sit still and quiet and spend a few moments being with God, saying slowly and silently in your mind, '*Be still and know that I am God.*'

❖

Imagine the fishermen folding their nets in the boat by the rocks. Picture the blue lake and the yellow sand, and the young woman standing on the hillside… Listen as she calls them, and hear what they say to Isaac. Watch them as they climb up the hillside.

See Isaac sit down and hurl a stone across the sand. Think about how he is feeling…

Now follow Isaac as he climbs up the hillside and down to the great crowd of people. Look at them as they press forward down to the water's edge. Notice Jesus, sitting in a boat near the shore… Watch Isaac searching for Peter. Picture Peter holding back the crowd. See Isaac run towards him. Wonder what Isaac is thnking. Wonder what Peter is thinking…

Listen to Isaac and Peter as they sit on the bank. Hear Peter roar with laughter… Listen to Peter as he talks about Jesus. Think how he is feeling. Think how Isaac is feeling…

Go with Isaac as he wades through the water. See him climb into Jesus' boat and hide. Watch the boats as they sail on to the open lake…

Feel the boat pitch and roll on the water. Hear the thunder crack and the waves crash over the bow… Picture James and John clinging to the sail. See Isaac struggle to his feet and fall down. Watch the lightning light up the lake and the figure of Jesus… Look at Jesus asleep on the cushion. Notice Isaac staring at him. Think how Isaac is feeling…

Watch Peter seize hold of the ropes. See him turn his head and look at Isaac. Go with him as he stumbles forward to Jesus. Think about how he is feeling. Think how Isaac is feeling…

Picture Jesus as he stands up. See him turn his face to the wind and cry out 'Peace!' See him spread his hands towards the water and cry 'Be still!' Feel the silence as calm settles on the water…

Watch Jesus as he looks at his disciples. Listen to him say, 'Do you still have no trust in me?' Think how Jesus is feeling. Think how his disciples are feeling…

Follow Peter and Isaac as they go to sit down. Listen to what

Isaac says. Listen to what Peter says. Think how Jesus has made them feel.

✤

Now sit in silence for a few moments more and think about what God is saying to you through the story. Think about how you feel. Think about what you would like to say to God and to Jesus. Thank God for his love.

## Questions for reflection

- Who were you in the prayer journey through the story?
- What did you think about how Isaac was feeling at the beginning of your prayer journey?
- How did you feel when you saw Isaac run towards Peter?
- What did you think when you heard what Peter said about Jesus?
- Describe how you felt when the storm began.
- Did you feel like Isaac when you saw Jesus asleep on the cushion?
- What did you think when you saw Peter let go of the ropes and stumble to Jesus?
- What was it like to see Jesus calm the wind and the waves? Could you feel the silence afterwards?
- How did you feel when you heard Jesus say, 'Do you still have no trust in me?'
- What did you think when you heard Isaac talking to Peter at the end of your prayer journey?
  - What do you think Jesus is saying to you? What do you want to say to him?

1. Use your prayer journal. Write down what you saw, heard, felt and did during your prayer journey. Use the *Questions for reflection* to help you if you want.

2. Read the story in your Bible. Read it slowly and carefully. Read it more than once. Listen to the words, and if a word or sentence draws your attention, hold it in your mind. Think over it silently—dwell on it until it sinks deep into your heart. Carry it with you into whatever you are doing for the rest of the day.

3. Paint a picture of the storm on the lake.

4. What makes you feel afraid? What do you do when you feel afraid, and why?

5. In New Testament times, the Greek word for fish was 'ichthys', and the fish was an early Christian symbol. Find out why. Make an 'ichthys' in relief. Draw the outline of a fish on plain paper. Write the Greek letters for 'ichthys' (ΙΧΘΥΣ) inside. Put a piece of aluminium foil, shiny side down, on a newspaper. Lay your fish picture on the top. Draw over the lines carefully with a blunt pencil or biro.

**Prayer**

Lord, I want to trust you, but I need your help. Show me that you're with me. Teach me, Lord, to see that even in my darkest hour, you are there with me.

# Freedom fighters and Romans

Jesus and his disciples arrived on the other side of Lake Galilee, in the territory of Gerasa. As soon as Jesus got out of the boat, he was met by a man who came out of the burial caves there. This man had an evil spirit in him and lived among the tombs.

**Mark 5:1–20**

 **Key verses: 1–3a**

# Introduction

Wherever Jesus is, he brings healing. He faced a violent madman, calm and unafraid, and brought peace into his heart and mind. As Jacob and Silas watched this happen, they were amazed by the power of God's love.

## Story

'And Jacob can be a Roman,' declared Silas, as he finished choosing sides for the game of 'Freedom Fighters against Romans'.

'But I'm always a Roman,' Jacob complained. 'Why can't I be a freedom fighter for a change?'

Silas jumped down from the whitewashed wall where he had been giving out his orders, sauntered over to Jacob and stabbed a short, stubby finger in the middle of his chest.

'I'll tell you why,' he grunted. 'Because your nose is as big as a Roman's, you smell like a Roman, and because I say so.'

The group of boys standing round them, who had run, leaping and whooping, from their lessons in the synagogue that morning, sniggered uneasily. No one argued with Silas if they knew what was good for them. Jacob should know that by now.

For one long moment the two boys stared each other in the eye, then Jacob looked away, his cheeks flushed red under his olive skin. Silas grinned. He turned to the others and winked broadly, then turned back to where Jacob squatted now on the ground, making patterns in the dirt with a stone.

Running his hands through his wiry hair, Silas frowned deeply, as if he was thinking something over. 'You know, Jacob,' he began slowly, 'to be a freedom fighter you've got to be very brave. After all, they are the ones who are trying to set us free from the Romans.'

The other boys muttered and nodded in agreement. Jacob lifted his head and gazed beyond them to the rocky hills that lay behind the whitewashed houses of the village.

'I am brave,' he declared. 'But you never give me the chance to prove it.'

'All right, then.' Silas folded his arms and winked at the others again. 'I'll give you the chance. Come to the madman's caves with me, tonight.'

'To... to the madman's caves... tonight?' Jacob bit his bottom lip and shuddered. 'I... I don't know if I should,' he said quickly. 'My father said to stay away from there. That madman's dangerous.'

Silas threw back his head and snorted. 'You're scared. Scaredy-cat! I knew it. How could you be a freedom fighter?'

Instantly Jacob sprang to his feet and Silas stepped backwards in surprise. 'I'm not a scaredy-cat,' he insisted. 'I will go with you. I'll show you I can be just as brave a freedom fighter as you.'

It was well after midnight when the two boys met at the edge of the village and began the slow climb over the rocks and boulders, towards the caves where the dead were buried and the madman lived alone. Darkness enveloped them like a cloak as the moon flitted behind a cloud at the first opportunity and not a single star pricked the black sky with light. Following Silas' tall figure as it trudged in front of him, Jacob turned his father's words of warning about the madman over and over in his head.

'It's not his fault, you understand. They say that something terrible happened to his family and drove him mad. He thinks he's full of devils that make him do bad things. Well, I don't know about that, but he's wild and fierce as a lion and so strong that chains can't hold him.'

Jacob knew that this was true. Once, some men had tried to chain the madman up, to stop him from rushing out of the caves at people as they passed by. But he had whipped himself into a frenzy and, with the strength of a great ox, had broken free and charged up the hillside, screeching. Jacob shivered as if he could hear the wild shrieks of the madman cutting shrilly through the cold night air.

He quickened his pace to catch up with Silas and fell in silently beside him. At the top of the low cliffs that overhung the sandy slope leading down to Lake Galilee, they stopped to get their breath. The limestone rock underneath was a honeycomb of dark caves and it was here that grieving relatives came to bury their dead.

'Right,' whispered Silas, pulling his cloak tightly around his shoulders. 'That's where he lives, in the caves down there.' He put one hand on Jacob's arm and gripped it tightly. 'Are... are you sure you want to go on?' His voice shook and he gripped Jacob even tighter. 'We can go back if you want... right now... I won't say anything to the others.'

Jacob peered at Silas intently through the dwindling darkness. Dawn was breaking now and shimmering fingers of light had begun to touch the waves that washed wearily over the yellow shore.

Silas was afraid. Jacob knew it. Big-headed, bossy, bullying Silas was scared. Jacob gulped in a mouthful of cold morning air and heaved himself up to his full height. He was afraid too, but he was not going to show it.

'Of course I want to go on,' he said firmly.

Silas released the grip on his arm and shrugged. 'OK, then, Mr Freedom Fighter,' he muttered and, walking forward, he beckoned Jacob to follow him as he started to pick his way slowly through the clumps of dried grass and stones.

Now standing, now squatting, the two boys stumbled and slithered on the gritty sand towards the caves below. Almost at the entrance, Silas stood up, shook the sand from his tunic, turned to look for Jacob and struck his heel on the edge of a sharp rock.

'Ah… ee… ee…' he shrieked at the top of his voice, then fell backwards, rolling down the slope until a thorn bush caught his cloak and brought him to a halt.

Suddenly a raw yell rent the air. A naked man rushed out of the caves towards them, bellowing like a mad bull. He was tall and skinny, his hair and beard matted with blood. His arms and legs were a mass of scars and sores, where he had cut himself in anguish on the sharp rocks and stones. The madman came at them, his empty eyes wide and terrified, and grabbed Silas by the shoulders as he lay quaking on the ground.

Jacob picked up a stone and threw it. And another and another. The madman let go of Silas and swivelled round to stare at him with bloodshot eyes. It was then that they heard the voices.

A boat had beached on the strip of shore and a group of men were climbing out. One man, who seemed to be their leader, walked on alone in front of all the others. Suddenly, at the sight of him, the madman began bounding down the slope, screaming and shouting so loudly that the cliffs rang out with the sound of his voice.

Silas scrambled to his feet and the two boys hid behind a rock and watched to see what the man would do.

'I hope he calls the other men to catch that lunatic,' muttered Silas. 'I hope there's a fight. I hope they beat him up, just like the freedom fighters would if they caught a Roman.'

'He can't help it,' insisted Jacob. 'It's not his fault he's gone mad. My father says…'

Silas snorted contemptuously. 'Your father! What does your father know?'

'My father…' Jacob's words froze in his mouth and he stared down the slope in amazement.

The leader of the group had raised his hand, and the madman lurched to a stop, yelled the name 'Jesus' at the top of his voice and fell down at the man's feet.

Silas whistled. 'That man—their leader—Jesus, his name must be. He didn't turn. He didn't run. He didn't fight.'

'He didn't need to,' said Jacob. 'He isn't afraid like everybody else. Look at him.'

Jesus stood silently on the hard, sandy grass. The first pale rays of the rising sun had fallen across his back and bathed him in light. Over on the beach, the other men seemed paralysed with fear, but Jesus gazed down into the tormented, upturned face of the man at his feet and spoke calmly, in a voice full of love.

'What is your name?' he asked.

The two boys strained to hear the madman's reply, but he was gabbling so quickly that they could not catch his words. Then Jesus said something in a sharp voice that sounded like a command.

Instantly, the madman was silent. And at that moment, so it seemed to Jacob and Silas, the whole world was silent. The madman sank down at Jesus' feet. The men on the beach stood rooted in the sand. The wind and the waves were hushed as a strange peace fell softly all about them.

Then, suddenly, the silence was shattered. The screaming began again and the two boys shot to their feet in fright. But this time it came from the top of the cliffs, where a man was tending a herd of pigs.

'It's the pigs!' cried Silas, pointing up the hill in horror. 'They've gone mad!'

The screaming got louder and louder. The whole herd was stampeding to the edge of the cliffs and the pigs were jumping, shrieking and squealing, into the water. Then, just as suddenly as it had started, the screaming stopped. All the pigs had drowned.

Silence fell again and still the naked madman sat, calm and unmoving. Two of the men on the beach edged forward slowly now and offered the man some clothes. They washed him in the sea and dressed him and then he went back to Jesus, and sat down in front of him again.

Silas shook his head in wonder as he gazed at Jesus. 'It's amazing,' he gasped. 'It's as if the madness went out of the madman and into the pigs.'

'Perhaps it did,' said Jacob. 'Look at him, he seems calm and as normal as you and me now.'

'They're not calm,' said Silas, pointing up the hill again at a group of men coming scrambling down towards them.

'Get out of the way!' they shouted at the two boys as they rushed angrily towards Jesus.

'We know what you did to our pigs!' they shouted. 'Go away! Get into your boat and leave. We don't want you here.'

Jesus said nothing. He turned to get into his boat, but the man who used to be mad caught hold of his cloak and begged him to take him too.

Jesus shook his head. 'No,' he said. 'Go home and tell everyone what God has done for you.'

The men pushed their boat off the shore and out on to the calm blue lake. Jacob and Silas stood to watch them go, then turned and climbed wearily back up the hill.

'Thank you for saving me from the madman,' muttered Silas as they reached the top. 'You are brave, Jacob, much braver than me.'

'Now can I be a freedom fighter?' asked Jacob.

Silas shook his head. 'No more Freedom Fighters and Romans. We don't need to fight to prove we're brave, do we? Jesus didn't fight. Jesus wasn't afraid. Jesus just showed God's love.'

Jacob looked at Silas in amazement. 'Jesus said, "Tell everyone what God has done for you."' He shook his head in wonder. 'And I will.'

## Look in

In a moment, you are going to close your eyes and imagine the world of the story as if you were there. Become part of it. You can be yourself or one of the boys, or anyone in the story you want to be. Picture yourself there, then move through the story in your imagination as the person you have chosen to be. Or, if you prefer, you can imagine you are trying to describe what is happening to someone else.

✤

Now, close your eyes, sit up straight and put your hands on your knees. Keep your body still, as this helps your mind to be still and concentrate as you go on your prayer journey. Take a deep breath and relax. Sit still and quiet and spend a few moments being with God, saying slowly and silently in your mind, *'Be still and know that I am God.'*

♣

Imagine the village where Jacob and Silas live. It's a hot day. Sunlight is shimmering on the whitewashed walls of the flat-roofed houses… Picture Silas sitting on the wall. Watch him jump down. Listen to him as he talks to Jacob. Think about how Jacob is feeling…

Now follow the boys at night as they climb over the rocks and boulders towards the caves. It's a cold, dark night with not a single star in the sky… See them stop at the top of the cliffs. Watch Silas as he pulls his cloak around his shoulders. Listen to what he says to Jacob. Think about how he is feeling…

Picture the boys slithering on the sand down to the caves. See Silas fall backwards and roll down the slope… Imagine the madman rushing out of the caves. Hear him yelling. See him grab Silas. Wonder how the madman feels…

Look at Jesus as he walks up the beach. See the madman run towards him. Hear him screaming and shouting… Listen to Silas and Jacob as they watch Jesus. Think about how Silas feels about the madman. Think about how Jacob feels…

See Jesus raise his hand. Watch the madman fall at his feet. Picture Jesus gazing into his face. Hear his voice ask, 'What is your name?' … Now listen to Jesus giving the man an order. Feel the silence that falls all around…

Watch Jacob and Silas jump to their feet. Listen to the pigs squealing. See them jump off the cliffs into the water…

Notice the madman sitting quietly on the beach. Watch the two men wash and dress him… Listen to the boys talk about the pigs. See the men come rushing down the hill at Jesus. Think about how they feel…

Follow Jesus as he gets into the boat. Listen to what the man who used to be mad says to him. Think how the man feels... Hear Jesus say, 'Tell everyone what God has done for you.' ...

Listen to Jacob and Silas as they climb up the hill. Think how Jesus has made them feel.

✣

Now sit in the silence for a few moments more and think about what God is saying to you through the story. Think about how you feel. Think about what you would like to say to God and to Jesus. Thank God for his love.

## Questions for reflection

- ❂ Who were you in the prayer journey through the story?
- ❂ What did you think when you heard Silas talking to Jacob at the beginning of your prayer journey?
- ❂ Describe how you felt when the madman came rushing out of the caves.
- ❂ Did you feel like Silas about the madman, or did you feel like Jacob? Why?
- ❂ What did you think when the madman fell down at Jesus' feet?
- ❂ Could you feel the peace when the madman was silent? What was it like?
- ❂ How did you feel when you saw the pigs jumping into the water?
- ❂ What did you think when you heard Silas talking to Jacob at the end of your prayer journey?
- ❂ What do you think Jesus is saying to you? What do you want to say to him?

1. Use your prayer journal. Write down what you saw, heard, felt and did during your prayer journey. Use the *Questions for reflection* to help you if you want.

2. Read the story in your Bible. Read it slowly and carefully. Read it more than once. Listen to the words, and if a word or sentence draws your attention, hold it in your mind. Think over it silently—dwell on it until it sinks deep into your heart. Carry it with you into whatever you are doing for the rest of the day.

3. Draw or paint a picture to express what you have felt or experienced.

4. Sit quietly and listen to the sounds that surround you. For five minutes, write down the different sounds that you hear. Think about the sounds that you hear every day, at home, in the garden, at school, going to the shops. Which sounds do you like? Which sounds don't you like? Why?

5. Make two peace hands. Draw round your hand twice and cut out the shapes. On the fingers of one hand, write all the ways in which the world could be made more peaceful. On the fingers of the other hand, write all the ways in which your home, school and friendships could be made more peaceful. Together with the rest of the children in your class, use your peace hands to make a peace tree on your classroom wall.

**Prayer**

Jesus, help us to open our hearts and minds to the peace and the power of your love. Amen

# Jairus' daughter

When Jesus had again crossed over by boat to the other side of the lake, a large crowd gathered round him while he was by the lake. Then one of the synagogue rulers, named Jairus, came there. Seeing Jesus, he fell at his feet and pleaded earnestly with him, 'My little daughter is dying. Please come and put your hands on her so that she will be healed and live.' So Jesus went with him.

**Mark 5:21–43**

 **Key verses: 21–24a (NIV)**

# Introduction

When a situation seems hopeless, it's hard to go on believing in God and not to be afraid. But God can do more than we can ever imagine. Joanna persevered for the sake of her friend and discovered that what looks impossible to us is possible with God.

# Story

Joanna hesitated in the open doorway, a jug of water clasped firmly in her hand, and peered into the darkened bedroom. Over by the wall, her master Jairus and his wife were sitting beside a small bed, where their daughter Lydia lay tossing and moaning.

'Come on, girl, hurry up,' beckoned the doctor who was bending over Lydia, with an impatient wave of his hand.

Joanna walked as quickly and as carefully as she could towards the bed, trying desperately not to spill one drop. The doctor took the jug, poured some water into a cup, added something from a bottle and nodded at Lydia's mother to lift her daughter's head. Lydia groaned and opened her eyes briefly as the doctor tried to force the cup between her lips.

'It's no good, doctor,' said Jairus in a low, weary voice. 'She won't take it. Day after day we sit here and she just seems to grow worse.'

'Every breath she takes is an effort,' whispered his wife. 'There must be something we can do, someone who can help...' Choking on the sobs that rose painfully in her throat, she buried her head in her arms and wept silently.

Joanna listened in agony. Her master and mistress were good people who treated all their servants well. Jairus was one of the most important and respected men in the town. A ruler of the synagogue, he used his power wisely—strict but just, no one ever questioned his authority lightly.

His daughter Lydia was a caring, gentle girl, who treated Joanna like a friend, and Joanna loved her. Now Lydia was sick, and Joanna felt certain she was dying. All of a sudden, she knew what she must do. Fearful and trembling, her heart pounding against her chest, she went and knelt at Jairus' feet.

'M-m-master,' Joanna stammered. 'There's a man, a healer— Jesus, his name is.'

'How dare you bother your master at a time like this?' snarled the doctor.

Jairus looked tired and grey. He stared at Joanna, then rested his hand lightly on her head. 'All right, Joanna, all right,' he mumbled. 'Back to your work now. Off you go.'

Outside in the courtyard, Joanna leant dejectedly against the whitewashed wall of the house, thoughts of Lydia racing inside her head. Jesus could make her well, she knew it. Joanna had heard about him first from the other servants, and then had seen him for herself, teaching and healing down by Lake Galilee. She had to make her master send for Jesus. But how?

It had taken all Joanna's courage to speak to Jairus just now and he had not listened, so what would be the good of going to speak to him again? In despair, Joanna slid on to the ground and closed her eyes against the piercing white of the sun. Pictures of Lydia, thin and pale, moved like shadows slowly through her mind.

Abruptly, Joanna sat up. 'I'm going to tell my master that he must find Jesus,' she said out loud, 'even if I'm punished.'

She found Jairus standing in the doorway, his empty eyes fixed on the worried back of the doctor, who was hurrying away down the street. Joanna crept up behind him, shaking and terrified at what she was about to do.

'Master,' she said. Jairus turned. 'This person, Jesus,' she plunged in quickly, 'he makes blind men see and cures lepers, he…'

Jairus' eyes filled with anger. 'Jesus, the carpenter,' he said in an iron voice. 'That dangerous troublemaker, who stirs up the people. I've been told about him.'

'But he can heal,' insisted Joanna. 'He can heal. I've seen him with my own eyes,' she cried, her desperation erupting in a storm of words that sent her master reeling. 'Men, women, children...'

'Stop!' Jairus raised his voice and his hand. 'That's enough.'

Joanna fell at his feet, all fear forgotten now in her love for Lydia. 'Jesus can heal mistress Lydia,' she said. 'I know he can. Go and see him for yourself.'

'That's enough, I said,' spluttered Jairus. 'How dare you speak to me like that?'

For a moment, Jairus loomed over her, his hand in the air. Then he gazed into her upturned, faithful face, full of concern for his daughter, and shook his head.

'Perhaps... perhaps he can,' he whispered and, lowering his hand, he pulled Joanna gently to her feet.

'Come,' he beckoned, his voice tight with urgency. 'I'm told he's down by Lake Galilee still.'

A crowd had gathered along the shore, getting thicker by the minute, pushing and jostling as people tried desperately to catch a glimpse of Jesus. Jairus and Joanna pressed their way through the throng, ignoring the clamouring voices calling Jesus' name, the sobbing of the sick, the smells, the dust, the persistent buzzing of the flies.

'Let me through!' ordered Jairus. 'I must get to Jesus. Let me through.'

Seeing Jairus, the crowd let them pass, and presently they found themselves face to face with Jesus and his disciples. Immediately, Jairus threw himself at Jesus' feet.

'My little daughter is dying. Please come and lay your hands on her, so she will get well and live,' he begged.

Joanna was astounded to see her master, the ruler of the synagogue, fall at Jesus' feet. But Jairus was in such despair that Jesus simply helped him up and turned to follow him home at once.

'Get out of our way! Please! My daughter's dying,' Jairus implored the crowd as he ploughed back through them.

Still, men and women pressed in on Jesus, clutching at him with their hot hands as he tried to follow Jairus. Then suddenly, Jesus stopped. Unaware, Jairus elbowed his way forward anxiously.

'Master, wait!' Joanna yelled after him. 'Master!'

Jairus turned. There was a sudden hush as the crowd came to a complete halt. Jesus was looking at the people standing behind him, his eyes searching their faces.

'Who touched my clothes?' Joanna heard him ask.

One of the disciples, a broad-shouldered fisherman, said, 'Master, you can see how people are crushing and pressing against you. What's the point of asking who touched you?'

'Someone touched me. I know that power went out of me,' Jesus insisted in a tired voice. His face was pale and his dark eyes looked exhausted.

Then Joanna saw a thin, bent woman stumble forward and kneel at his feet. In a tearful voice, she admitted that she was the one who had touched him; then she poured out such a torrent of words that Joanna could only catch the last thing she said. 'So I touched your cloak, and I was healed.'

Jesus laid his hand gently on the woman's shoulder. 'Daughter,' he said, 'your faith has healed you. Go in peace.'

At that moment, Joanna turned back to Jairus. Two men were standing next to him, their faces drawn and grey. Joanna froze, cold as ice, as she heard them say, 'Your daughter is dead. Why bother the teacher any more?'

Jairus closed his eyes; he gave a deep, despairing moan and his whole body began to shake. Instantly, Jesus was beside him. 'Don't be afraid! Only keep on believing,' Jesus told him urgently.

The crowd broke like waves against a hard rock as Jesus took Jairus by the arm and led him through. Joanna stumbled after them, blinded by her tears, weighed down by the thought that Lydia had died and they had not been with her.

It was all her fault, she told herself. If only she had behaved as she should, had kept quiet, then her master would have been with his daughter and not with Jesus. And what use was Jesus now? she asked herself angrily as she brushed the tears away with the back of her hand. Lydia was dead.

Even before they reached the house, they could hear people weeping and wailing loudly. Friends and neighbours had gathered downstairs to grieve, crying and chanting so that the whole house sang with the noise of sadness.

Jesus allowed no one to go any further with him, except three of his disciples—Peter, James and John. He entered the house, stopped and spoke to the people inside.

'Why all this noise and weeping?' he asked. 'The child is not dead, she's sleeping.'

'Sleeping!' they muttered among themselves. 'Sleeping! The man's mad.'

Then they began to laugh scornfully at him, and Joanna almost laughed too. In a calm, determined voice, Jesus told them all to go. When they had gone, he went with Jairus and his wife, upstairs to Lydia's room. The three disciples followed.

Joanna crept after them and crouched against the wall. Inside the room, all was quiet until she heard Jesus say, 'Little girl, get up.'

'Get up?' Joanna said to herself. 'How can she?'

Then she heard Jairus and his wife gasp in astonishment and the sound of footsteps padding around the room.

'Now, give her something to eat,' Jesus' voice came again. 'And tell no one what's happened here.'

Joanna could contain herself no longer. Her heart racing wildly in her chest, she peered into the darkened room and saw Lydia sitting on the bed. Her master and mistress were sitting next to her, each with their arms around her, and Jesus was standing, looking on.

It was at that moment that Jesus turned quietly and began to walk out of the room. Joanna crouched back against the wall, joy bubbling up inside her, eyes as round and shining as the sun. Then Jesus came through the doorway and stopped in front of her. He smiled and her heart was moved with love.

'Give her something to eat,' he urged gently, and was gone.

Joanna stood in the courtyard, watching the sky darken as the day faded and the sun sank from view. Lydia was well now, and the whole house rang with the sound of rejoicing.

'Joanna!' Jairus' voice called from the doorway. Joanna spun round. 'I was angry when you spoke to me this morning,' he said.

Joanna stood like stone. She lowered her eyes and stared at her feet. Was she to be punished now for speaking out? she asked herself. Well, if she was, it was nothing. Lydia was alive and that was all that mattered.

Her master walked towards her. 'But now I want to say thank you for having the courage to make me listen,' he said. He touched her lightly on the arm, and Joanna stared at him in astonishment. 'It was hard to go on believing and not be afraid,

wasn't it?' he mused, shaking his head thoughtfully. 'But God can do more than we can ever imagine.'

Joanna nodded as Jairus walked back into the house. What had seemed to her impossible, Jesus had made possible.

What had seemed to her dead, he had brought to life.

## Look in

In a moment, you are going to close your eyes and imagine the world of the story as if you were there. Become part of it. You can be yourself, Joanna or Jairus, or anyone in the story you want to be. Picture yourself there, then move through the story in your imagination as the person you have chosen to be. Or, if you prefer, you can imagine you are trying to describe what is happening to someone else.

✤

Now, close your eyes, sit up straight and put your hands on your knees. Keep your body still, as this helps your mind to be still and concentrate as you go on your prayer journey. Take a deep breath and relax. Sit still and quiet and spend a few moments being with God, saying slowly and silently in your mind, *'Be still and know that I am God.'*

✤

Picture Joanna in the bedroom doorway. Jairus and his wife are sitting beside Lydia's bed. Lydia is moaning as the doctor bends over her... Watch Joanna take the jug to the doctor. See the doctor try to make Lydia drink. Listen to Jairus and his wife. Think about how they are feeling...

Look at Lydia as she kneels at Jairus' feet. Listen to what she says about Jesus. Listen to what the doctor and Jairus say...

Follow Joanna outside into the courtyard. Think about how she is feeling...

Watch Joanna as she goes to find Jairus. Listen to what she tells him about Jesus. Listen to what Jairus replies... Picture Jairus raising his hand in the air. See Joanna fall at his feet. Wonder what they are thinking... Watch Jairus pull Joanna to her feet.

Follow them as they go down to Lake Galilee... Imagine the desperate crowd. Picture Jairus and Joanna forcing their way through. See Jairus fall at Jesus' feet. Think how Jairus is feeling...

Go with Jairus and Jesus through the crowd. Notice Jesus stop suddenly. Look at him as his eyes search the crowd... Hear Jesus say, 'Power went out of me.' Think about how he is feeling... Watch as the woman kneels at his feet. Hear Jesus say, 'Your faith has healed you.' Wonder how the woman is feeling...

Listen to the two men standing with Jairus. Hear Jesus say, 'Don't be afraid!' Wonder how Jairus is feeling. Wonder how Joanna is feeling...

Follow Jesus and Jairus back to the house. Hear all the people weeping. Listen to what Jesus tells them... Go with Jesus and the others up to Lydia's room. See Joanna follow... Hear Jesus say, 'Little girl, get up.' Hear the footsteps padding around the room. Wonder what Joanna is thinking...

Watch Joanna peer into the room. See Jairus and his wife sitting with Lydia. Think about how they are feeling... Go with Jesus out of the room. Notice Joanna crouched against the wall. See Jesus smile at Joanna and say, 'Give her something to eat.' Think how Joanna is feeling...

Picture Jairus and Joanna outside in the courtyard. Listen to what they are saying. Think how Jesus has made them feel.

❖

Now sit in the silence for a few moments more and think about what God is saying to you through the story. Think about how you feel. Think about what you would like to say to God and to Jesus. Thank God for his love.

## Questions for reflection

- Who were you in the prayer journey through the story?
- What did you think when you heard Jairus and his wife talking at the beginning of your prayer journey?
- How did you feel when you heard Joanna try to talk to Jairus the second time?
- What did you think when you heard what Jairus said about Jesus?
- How did you feel when you saw Jairus fall at Jesus' feet?
- What did you think when you heard Jesus say, 'Power went out of me'?
- Describe how you felt when you heard the two men talking to Jairus.
- What did you think when you heard Jesus say, 'Little girl, get up'?
- How did you feel when you saw Jairus and his wife sitting with Lydia?
- How did you feel when you heard Jairus and Joanna talking at the end of your prayer journey?
  - What do you think Jesus is saying to you? What do you want to say to him?

## Look out

1. Use your prayer journal. Write down what you saw, heard, felt and did during your prayer journey. Use the *Questions for reflection* to help you if you want.

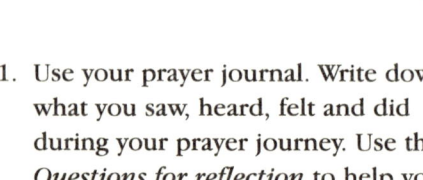

2. Read the story in your Bible. Read it slowly and carefully. Read it more than once. Listen to the words, and if a word or sentence draws your attention, hold it in your mind. Think over it silently—dwell on it until it sinks deep into your heart. Carry it with you into whatever you are doing for the rest of the day.

3. What does 'perseverance' mean? Do you know or have you heard about someone who persevered? Why did they do it?

4. Find a small branch and fix it in a plastic pot. Cut out leaf shapes from green paper. Write on each leaf one way in which you could help others. Make the branch come alive by hanging/sticking the leaves on it.

5. Draw a large 'gift' box for a friend on a piece of paper. Decorate it with designs, pictures or words that describe what their friendship means to you.

## Prayer

Dear God, sometimes it's hard to go on trying. Sometimes it's hard to go on believing. But you can do more than we can ever imagine. We praise you and thank you that everything is possible with you.

# The angry young man

When they arrived in Jerusalem, Jesus went to the Temple and began to drive out all those who were buying and selling.

**Mark 11:15–17**

**Key verse: 15a**

# Introduction

Sometimes we are so concerned with the things we have and the things we want that we shut God out. We forget about the things that really matter and become concerned only with ourselves. It took Jesus' anger to shock Susanna and her mother into thinking in a different way.

# Story

From their cramped wooden cages piled carelessly in the dimly lit courtyard, the pigeons blinked and stared at Susanna as she waited impatiently for her mother. Night had only just turned into day and the birds were beginning to coo and twitter. Restless and hungry, they tapped against the cages until Susanna could bear it no more. 'Be quiet, stupid birds,' she hissed. 'And keep still or you'll break your wings. Then no one will buy you and that means no new tunic and no new sandals for me.'

Glaring at the pigeons, she stared into their faces; and for a moment, to her amazement, it seemed as if their bright, sad eyes spoke to her of vast blue skies and rolling hills, of windswept trees and wild places. Susanna gasped softly. Slowly, she lifted a lid. Hesitantly, she watched the birds straighten and stretch their necks in the freedom of the cool morning air.

'Susanna!' a voice called. Susanna let the lid fall shut. 'It's time to go. The temple will be swarming with pilgrims up for the Passover festival. Best set the stall up before the crowds gather.' Susanna's mother bustled through the doorway and into the courtyard, tying a money-bag tightly around her thick waist. 'Pick up the cages, then, and let's be off. Business should be good today—plenty of families wanting to celebrate a new baby by offering a pair of pigeons to God.'

Small groups of pilgrims were already beginning to spill out on to the narrow streets of Jerusalem, Susanna noticed as she followed her mother. Up the steep hill towards the great temple they climbed, to the heart of the holy city itself.

'Hurry up, Susanna!' her mother urged. 'The sooner we get there, the sooner we can start selling. I've got my eye on some new cooking-pots, a fine cloak for your father and leather belts for your brothers, with the money we make today.' She stopped for a moment, breathless. 'Oh, and a mat for the house.'

The list was getting longer. Susanna was worried. 'And a new tunic for me,' she reminded her mother, 'and sandals.'

At last they reached the temple. Hurrying through the gate, they made their way over the great outer courtyard called the Court of the Gentiles, to where men and women were already setting out their wares. Her mother settled down behind an empty stall and Susanna crashed the cages thankfully to the floor.

'Careful, Susanna,' her mother moaned. 'Those pigeons are like gold.'

Gold, thought Susanna as she gazed around the courtyard. That was all the festival seemed to be about. Everywhere she looked, people were buying and selling, calling to the pilgrims who had begun to teem like ants through the temple gate.

Men who sold oxen, sheep and goats for the temple sacrifices shouted, 'Over here! Fine goats, get your goats here!' or 'Sheep for sale, sheep for sacrifice!'

Then her mother called out, 'Pigeons, perfect pigeons! Celebrate your new baby! Buy a pair of pigeons to give to God!'

Before long, every inch of space in the vast courtyard was crowded; the air was choked with the sounds of sheep bleating and goats braying and pigeons cooing. Men argued furiously over prices, bargained and haggled, dragged their frightened animals up and down, until the whole courtyard was nothing but a dirty, noisy, smelly, seething circus.

Susanna watched the money changers change ordinary money into temple money called shekels. All Jewish men paid a tax to the temple every year, and this had to be paid in shekels.

Often the money changers cheated, and men snarled, 'Snake' and 'Dog' at them under their breaths as they turned away.

'Stop gawking, Susanna, and give me a hand,' complained her mother, who was wrestling with a pigeon trying to escape. 'Priests!' she exploded, as she squashed it into a cage and shut the lid. 'Priests, wandering up and down with nothing better to do than interfere.'

She clenched the money-bag like a dagger between her hands. 'Did you hear that one with the angry face and the long beard? Said some of my pigeons weren't good enough to be offered to God. Weren't perfect.'

She pulled her mantle over her dark hair and whipped one end of it furiously across her shoulders. 'Not perfect! I'd like to know if those priests are perfect. Look at them, arguing and complaining, telling people they're charging too little or too much, letting anybody pass up and down, like the place was just a shortcut to the other side of the city or something and not a temple at all.' She stopped for breath and shook her head.

'Priests. It's their job to say prayers, and mine to sell pigeons.'

Susanna nodded in agreement. It was their job to say prayers, and particularly at Passover time, she supposed. But how could anyone pray in the middle of a noisy uproar such as this?

Susanna loved Passover. All the excitement of getting ready, the special Passover meal, the telling of the Passover story by her father. A hush, unbroken as a seamless cloak, fell over the whole family when he told them again how the Jewish people had been delivered by God from their slavery in Egypt and led to freedom by Moses.

'A pair of pigeons for Passover, lady?' her mother's voice cut through her thoughts. 'What a lovely baby. Boy, is it? Have a good Passover,' she said, stuffing the silver coin into the mouth of her bag. 'A good Passover. Huh. What's that? More expense. More hard work. Cleaning, cooking, shopping.' She caught Susanna's eye. 'It's a good job business is brisk, my girl. Let's hope we sell the lot.'

Susanna was just beginning to feel hungry when the figure of a tall young man, standing in the middle of the milling crowd, caught her eye. He stood upright and unmoving, as though he had been

turned to stone, but his face wore a look of disgust and his eyes blazed with such anger that Susanna began to feel afraid. All around him, animals bleated and lowed in distress; traders called, pilgrims haggled, priests argued, and men trailed their dirty feet through the temple area, which should have been a place of prayer.

Then, suddenly, the young man bent over, seized a piece of rope from a stall and knotted it into a whip. Before anyone could stop him, he strode towards the money changers, put his hand under the corner of the first table he came to and flipped it over. Coins scattered everywhere, rolling and spinning around the floor. Children and men on their hands and knees scrambled after them. Holding the whip above his head, the young man brought it lashing down on to the next table, toppling it over sideways with the force of his blow.

'Hey, what do you think you're doing?' the money changers yelled at him. 'Someone call the temple guard. He's gone mad.'

Susanna clutched her mother's tunic. 'Who's that young man, and why is he turning over the tables like that?' she asked.

'I don't know why he's doing it,' her mother said. 'But I do know who he is. It's that Jesus fellow. From Nazareth. Some sort of a teacher and healer, so they say.'

Within minutes there was another crash. From out of nowhere priests came scuttling towards the uproar, the temple guard at their back. The young man stopped and faced them. Standing quite still, the calmness of his body was betrayed by the fire in his eyes. Uncertain what to do, the priests made a move towards him. Jesus raised the whip above his head and turned on them a look of such fury that it froze them, paralysed with fear, on the spot.

Silence spread like oil on water over the nervous crowd. Only the bleating of sheep and goats and the cooing of restless pigeons broke the sudden stillness.

Jesus raised the whip higher, stared out across the multitude of faces and shouted, 'Clear everything out! Stop making a market-place of God's temple! This is meant to be a house of prayer for all people, but you have turned it into a hideout for thieves.'

Guilt flickered for a moment across the grim faces of the

priests. Then one of them shook his fist at Jesus. 'Who gave you the right to do this?' he demanded.

Jesus took a step towards him. The priest backed away. There was another mighty crash as Jesus hurled over a stall selling oil and incense with just one hand. Then the crowd began to panic.

Men grabbed their animals and bolted, ducking and dodging to escape the whip that Jesus was using to clear the way. Priests raced up and down, tables toppled, money changers screamed, sheep and goats stampeded round and round.

'Let's get out of here, Susanna!' her mother yelled above the din.

Susanna picked up the cages. They were still heavy. Only half the pigeons that they had brought had been sold. She gave the cages a hard shake. 'No new tunic and no new sandals,' she muttered at them, 'and it's all the fault of that angry young man.'

'Quick, Susanna!' shrieked her mother. 'He's turned and he's coming this way.'

Jesus swept towards them, a whirlwind in the middle of a storm, and before they could stop him he was opening the cages and shaking the pigeons free. Susanna watched in horror. She put out a hand to stop him and his hand touched hers. Then Jesus bent his head. He searched her face with eyes full of sorrow; and for a moment, to her amazement, it seemed as if she saw the temple with his eyes.

Jesus kept his gaze fixed on Susanna's face as he picked up a cage and offered it to her. She stared at it, then fastened her eyes upon his. Immediately, Jesus smiled and his eyes spoke to her now of vast blue skies and rolling hills; of freedom, of Passover and of prayer.

Inside the cage, the pigeons cooed and twittered. Susanna lifted the lid. She tipped the cage over and shook it hard. Then another and another. Birds fluttered everywhere. Frantic with freedom, they flew into the air and hovered above the seething crowd. All at once, as if they were one, they rose together and shot like a feathered arrow towards the courtyard walls. Up they flew, circling the towers, fading like mist beyond the hot sun.

Susanna's heart felt as if it must explode with happiness as she watched the fleeing birds. Turning back to Jesus as they disappeared, she was dismayed to find that he had disappeared as well.

'Susanna, over here!' Her mother's voice made her jump.

Standing in the midst of a mound of empty cages, she was dabbing her eyes with the end of her mantle and sniffing loudly. Susanna slipped her arm around her mother's waist. The money-bag was half empty, she realized guiltily.

'Don't cry, mother,' she said. 'There'll be enough for your cooking-pots. I don't care about tunics and sandals, and...' she hesitated as she glanced at the sky, 'we can get more pigeons.'

Her mother shook her head. 'No,' she whispered. 'No more pigeons. When I saw those birds flying free like that, I thought, that's what Passover's about—freedom and thanksgiving, not money.' She stared around the temple courtyard, empty now of money changers, traders and animals. 'That young man was right. This is meant to be a house of prayer, not a market.' And she bowed her head, closed her eyes and prayed.

## Look in

In a moment, you are going to close your eyes and imagine the world of the story as if you were there. Become part of it. You can be yourself, Susanna or her mother, or anyone in the story you want to be. Picture yourself there, then move through the story in your imagination as the person you have chosen to be. Or, if you prefer, you can imagine you are trying to describe what is happening to someone else.

❖

Now, close your eyes, sit up straight and put your hands on your knees. Keep your body still, as this helps your mind to be still and concentrate as you go on your prayer journey. Take a deep breath and relax. Sit still and quiet and spend a few moments being with

God, saying slowly and silently in your mind, '*Be still and know that I am God.*'

Picture the dimly lit courtyard and the pile of cages. It's early in the morning. The hungry pigeons are noisy and restless… Listen to Susanna as she talks to the birds. Watch her stare into their faces. Think about how she is feeling… See her mother bustle through the doorway.

Now follow them as they climb up the hill to the temple. Listen to what they are saying…

Imagine Susanna's mother setting out the stall. Watch the money changers changing money. Look at the men selling sheep and goats. Hear the noise of the animals shrieking and the men shouting… Listen to Susanna's mother talking about the priests. Think about how she is feeling… Watch her now as she sells the pigeons. Hear what she says about Passover. Think how she is feeling. Think how Susanna is feeling…

See Jesus standing in the crowd. Notice the look in his eyes and the look on his face. Watch him seize some rope and make a whip. Go with him as he turns over the money changers' tables. Think how he is feeling…

Look at the priests as they run towards Jesus. See Jesus stop and face them. Listen to him say, 'This is meant to be a house of prayer for all people, but you have turned it into a hideout for thieves.' … Watch the priest shake his fist at Jesus. See Jesus take a step towards him. Wonder what the priests are thinking…

Picture the crowd begin to panic. Watch the sheep and goats racing round and round. Look at Jesus turning over tables. Hear the noise as they crash to the ground…

Listen to Susanna as she shakes the cages. See Jesus come towards her. Watch Jesus opening the cages. Think how Susanna is feeling… Watch Jesus look at Susanna. Watch Susanna look at Jesus. Think how Jesus feels. Think how Susanna feels… Look at Susanna freeing the pigeons.

Notice her mother with the empty cages. Listen to what Susanna says. Listen to what her mother says. Think how Jesus has made them feel.

❖

Now sit in the silence for a few moments more and think about what God is saying to you through the story. Think about how you feel, and what you would like to say to God and to Jesus.

## Questions for reflection

- Who were you in the prayer journey through the story?
- What did you think about how Susanna was feeling at the beginning of your prayer journey?
- What did you think when you heard her mother talking about the priests?
- How did you feel when you heard what her mother said about Passover?
- Describe how you felt when Jesus turned over the money changers' tables.
- What did you think when Jesus said, 'This is meant to be a house of prayer for all people, but you have turned it into a hideout for thieves'?
- What was it like to watch Jesus opening the cages?
- How did you feel when Jesus and Susanna looked at each other?
- What did you think when you heard Susanna and her mother talking at the end of your prayer journey?
- What do you think Jesus is saying to you? What do you want to say to him?

1. Use your prayer journal. Write down what you saw, heard, felt and did during your prayer journey. Use the *Questions for reflection* to help you if you want.
2. Read the story in your Bible. Read it slowly and carefully. Read it more than once. Listen to the words, and if a word or sentence draws your attention, hold it in your mind. Think over it silently—dwell on it until it sinks deep into your heart. Carry it with you into whatever you are doing for the rest of the day.
3. You can talk to God at any time—in bed when you wake in the morning; on your way to school; in the car or in the bus; at lunchtime. Make a list of 'prayer moments' throughout the day when you could enjoy being with God.
4. Create a prayer place, a special place to be with God. It could be in your bedroom, a corner of the lounge, your garden. You could put a Bible there or a cross, a picture or some flowers. Always come into your prayer place quietly and prayerfully.
5. Find out about the festival of Passover.

## Prayer

Dear God, help me not to be so busy doing and getting that I forget about you. Open my eyes and my heart to the glory of your love. Amen

# The dinner guest

Then Jesus said to his host, 'When you give a lunch or a dinner, do not invite your friends or your brothers or your relatives or your rich neighbours—for they will invite you back, and in this way you will be paid for what you did. When you give a feast, invite the poor, the crippled, the lame, and the blind; and you will be blessed, because they are not able to pay you back.'

**Luke 14:12–24**

 **Key verses: 12–14a**

# Introduction

Every one of us is important to God. He cares for each of us individually. We are special to him. He knows our names. Jesus said that not one single sparrow is forgotten by God and we are more valuable to him than a great many sparrows. He loves us more than we can imagine and invites us all to come to him. Jesus told a story about God's invitation, and Esther couldn't wait to accept.

# Story

'Hurry up and fill those water-pots, girl! The master's invited a special guest to dinner, Jesus the teacher, and everything must be ready,' shouted Ebenezer the head servant as he shuffled, back bent, out of the courtyard.

Esther wiped her hands down the front of her dress and shrugged. What did it matter to her who the master invited? Taking a deep breath, she lifted the jug of water and carefully filled three large clay bowls.

'Anything else while I'm at it?' she muttered to herself. 'Fill those water-pots, girl. Find the plates, girl. Fetch the bread, girl.' Esther shook her head. 'Girl, girl, girl. Doesn't Ebenezer know I've got a name? Stupid old man! He's only a servant like me, after all.'

She put the water jug down and stared after him. Being head servant in the house of Matthew the Pharisee, one of the most important men in Jerusalem, was not easy, she knew. But it seemed to Esther that all Ebenezer ever did was give orders, while she had to do all the work.

One by one, the dinner guests came in through the courtyard. Esther's master, Matthew, greeted them and sent them to stretch out on the cushions and mats set comfortably beside the low table. When they had all arrived, at a signal from Ebenezer, who was leaning on a stick and frowning in the shadow of the dining-room wall, Esther began to serve them in turn.

Backwards and forwards she trotted, up and down, ears tuned to the string of orders that shot from Ebenezer's tongue. 'Bring the wine, girl. More bread over here, girl. Where's the chicken, girl?'

The guests were talking loudly now and the harsh hum of their voices hung on the air. But Esther was too busy to listen to what they were saying, too tired even to try. At last she shrank back against the wall exhausted, as cups were drained and empty plates pushed away. Ebenezer leaned over his stick towards her, his face worn and grey, his mouth open as if to say, 'Girl!' yet again. Instead, he shook his head wearily, shrank back against the wall as well and thankfully closed his eyes.

Now the room hushed slowly to silence and the guests settled down into their cushions like well-fed cats. Then Esther heard the man sitting next to her master, the man they called Jesus, say, 'Next time you give a dinner, don't just invite your friends and family and rich neighbours, because they will invite you back. Instead, invite people who never get invited out—the poor, the crippled and the blind. They won't be able to repay you, but God will.'

Matthew the Pharisee looked annoyed. Esther shook her head and grinned. The cheek of it, she thought, telling her master whom to invite to his own house. Not that she could imagine him ever inviting the sort of people Jesus had suggested, of course. Mind you, he did give to the poor, and the exact amount he was supposed to, no more and no less.

All the other men around the table looked annoyed as well. They propped themselves up on their elbows and watched Jesus as he began to speak again, their eyes glittering like hawks. One of them, the man sitting opposite him, leaned forward across the empty plates and sighed, 'How happy you would be if you were fortunate enough to sit down to dinner in God's kingdom.'

Jesus nodded. 'There was once a rich man...' he began.

'There was once a rich man... there was once a rich man...'

In the heavy heat of the late afternoon, the words swam round and round inside Esther's head until she felt as if she was drowning. Jesus was telling a story.

Esther sighed. Her mother used to tell her stories years ago, but she had died when Esther was small. Frowning, she tried to recall her mother's face, but it was no good. All she could remember from her childhood, when she was first brought to the Pharisee's house and put to work, was her master's face, peering down at her, asking who she was.

'Now the rich man was planning to have a huge party,' Jesus went on, his strong, clear voice pulling Esther back from the whirlpool of her dreams. 'He had made a long list of all the people he was going to invite. His servants worked hard preparing the food. They decided where everyone should sit around an enormous table and they decorated the room with flowers.

'When everything was ready, the rich man called to one of his servants. "Here's a list of all my friends who are coming to

the party. Run round to their houses and tell them that everything is ready."

"'Yes of course," said the servant, "I'll be as quick as I can."

'The servant thought that everyone would be waiting in their
best clothes, ready to come. But he had a surprise.'

Jesus paused. His eyes swept the circle of guests at the table,
and the other men leaned forward, spellbound, waiting for him
to go on. Brushing the hair away from his damp forehead, he
picked up a cup of water and drained it dry.

At that moment, peeping like a mouse out of the shadows,
Esther's eyes met his. And Jesus smiled. Jesus smiled as if he knew
her... as if he knew all about her... as if he knew who she was.

Suddenly Esther wanted to sing. She wanted to dance. She
wanted to run across the room to Jesus and fling herself into his
arms. Instead, she heaved a deep sigh, clenched her fists tightly
by her side and listened in anticipation as he started to speak
again.

'The servant came to the house of the first friend on the list.
He knocked loudly on the door. The door opened. "I've just
come to tell you that my master's party is ready," he said.

"'Oh, I can't come now," said the man. "I've bought a new
field today and I'm just going to see what it's like."

'That's a poor excuse, thought the servant. Fancy buying a
field without looking at it first.

'And away he went to the second house. He knocked loudly
on the door. The door opened. "I've just come to tell you that my
master's party is ready," he said. ·

"'Oh, I can't come now," said the man. "I've just bought five
pairs of oxen to work on my farm. I must go and try them out."

'That's a poor excuse, thought the servant. Fancy buying five
pairs of oxen without trying them out first.

'And away he went to the third house. He knocked loudly on
the door. The door opened. "I've just come to tell you that my
master's party is ready," he said.

"'Oh, I can't come now," said the man. "I've just got married
and I can't leave my wife."

'That's a poor excuse, thought the servant. Fancy not going to a party just because you've got married.

'And away he went. The servant went to every house on the list. Everyone was busy. Nobody would come. He went back to tell his master.'

Slowly, Jesus' voice tapered away into silence and a hush fell on the room, broken only by the faint buzz of a fly as it flitted from plate to plate. Esther willed Jesus to go on, desperate to know what the rich man would say, furious with all the friends who had refused his invitation. Some friends! Why, if Esther was invited to a party (not that she ever would be, of course), she certainly wouldn't refuse.

Jesus sat up straight at the table. He thrust his chin out, stroked his beard, then folded his arms. Esther giggled. Now he looked just like she imagined the rich man would, standing at the door ready to receive all his friends.

'Well,' Jesus continued, 'the rich man was standing at the door of his beautiful home, waiting to welcome his guests.

'"Where are they?" he asked when his servant appeared. "Everything's ready and I can't wait to start."

'"They're not coming," said the servant. "They've all got other things to do."

'The rich man was furious. "What rude, bad-mannered people," he said. He went inside and looked at the tables, full of delicious food. "I know what I'll do," he said. "Go out into the town. Look in all the streets. Look for the sort of people who never get asked to anybody's party. Look for poor people, sick people, beggars and tramps. Ask them all to come. If you can't find enough poor people in the town, go out into the country as well. I want lots of people to come. We'll have a wonderful party."

'The servant rushed off again. Almost at once he saw an old man begging for money in the street. "Come with me to my master's party," he said. "He specially wants you to come."

'"Nobody's ever asked me to a party," said the old man. "You must be joking. He can't want me to come."

'"Oh yes he does," said the servant. "Come on."

'And off they went together. Just a little further down the road, the servant saw a woman who was blind. "Come with me to my master's party," he said. "He specially wants you to come."

'"Nobody's ever asked me to a party," said the woman. "You must be joking. He can't want me to come."

'"Oh yes he does," said the servant. "Come on."

'And so the servant asked all the people he could find. Soon the road was crowded with the poor and the sick coming to the party. The rich man looked out of his window. He saw the people walking down the road towards his house. Everyone seemed happy and excited. The rich man opened his door wide.

'"Come in, come in," he shouted. "There's room for you all. Now my party is full of people who really want to be here, and none of those I invited first will get anything to eat at all."'

The story was over. For a moment, silence fell. Presently, from around the table came the sound of coughs and grunts as guests began to look away from Jesus and mutter among themselves. 'What's he getting at?' they asked each other in whispers.

But Esther did not look away from Jesus. She understood. Her eyes remained fixed on his face as the story sank deep into her heart. The invitation was to her and everyone like her. She really was wanted at the party.

'Stop daydreaming, Esther.' Ebenezer's gentle voice brought her slowly to her feet in amazement. He had called her by her name. 'That was a wonderful story. But this party's over, Esther, and there's work to be done,' he said.

A look of understanding passed between them, and the girl and the old man smiled, like good friends who hadn't seen each other for a long time. Ebenezer turned to go, and Esther made to follow him. At the door she stopped for a moment and looked back. Across the room, over empty plates and bent heads, Jesus' eyes, alight with love, met hers. And the look in his eyes said, 'Well, will you come to the party?'

'Yes,' she called to him in her heart, 'I'm coming.' She glanced through the open door at Ebenezer shuffling slowly towards the kitchen. 'We're coming. Save a place at the table for us.'

## Look in

In a moment, you are going to close your eyes and imagine the world of the story as if you were there. Become part of it. You can be yourself, a guest, Esther, or anyone in the story you want to be. Picture yourself there, then move through the story in your imagination as the person you have chosen to be. Or, if you prefer, you can imagine you are trying to describe what is happening to someone else.

✣

Now, close your eyes, sit up straight and put your hands on your knees. Keep your body still, as this helps your mind to be still and concentrate as you go on your prayer journey. Take a deep breath and relax. Sit still and quiet and spend a few moments being with God, saying slowly and silently in your mind, *'Be still and know that I am God.'*

❖

Picture the courtyard where Esther is filling the water-pots. It is cool and shady, with an archway leading into the Pharisee's house… Listen to Ebenezer as he talks to Esther. Watch him shuffle away. Think about how she is feeling…

Imagine the dining-room. See the low table with the cushions and mats set around it. Watch the guests as they stretch out…

Now follow Esther as she serves the guests. Listen to Ebenezer's orders. Smell the food as she brings it to the table… Feel how tired Esther is, how tired Ebenezer is, as they shrink back against the wall… Now look at the men around the table. Listen to Jesus telling them whom to invite to dinner. Wonder what the men are thinking…

Picture Esther as she listens to Jesus begin his story. Hear his strong, clear voice. Watch him as his eyes sweep around the circle of men. Look at his hands as he picks up the cup of water…

See Esther look at Jesus. See Jesus smile as if he knew her. Think about how that made her feel…

Listen to Jesus telling about the servant going to all the houses. Imagine how the servant felt when no one would come… Think about how this made Esther feel… Imagine Jesus stroking his beard and folding his arms. Hear him tell how the rich man sent his servant into the town. Watch the servant invite the beggar and the blind woman. Think about how they feel…

Picture the poor people and the sick people walking down the crowded road to the rich man's house. Look at their faces… Watch the rich man welcome them in…

See Esther look at Jesus as the story ends. Imagine how she

feels... Listen to Ebenezer say Esther's name. See them smile at each other... Picture Jesus looking at Esther. Hear him say 'Will you come to the party?' Hear Esther say, 'Yes'... See Esther watch Ebenezer. Hear her say, 'Save a place at the table for us.'

✤

Now sit in the silence for a few moments more and think about what God is saying to you through the story. Think about how you feel. Think about what you would like to say to God and to Jesus. Thank God for his love.

## Questions for reflection

- Who were you in the prayer journey through the story?
- How did you feel when you heard Ebenezer talking to Esther at the beginning of your prayer journey?
- What did you think when Jesus told the men at the table whom to invite to dinner?
- What was it like to hear Jesus telling a story?
- What did you think when you heard the rich man tell his servant to invite poor people, sick people and beggars to his party?
- How did you feel when you saw Jesus smile at Esther as if he knew her?
- What did you think Jesus was saying through his story?
- How did you feel when you heard Ebenezer talking to Esther at the end of your prayer journey?
- What do you think Jesus is saying to you? What do you want to say to him?

1. Use your prayer journal. Write down what you saw, heard, felt and did during your prayer journey. Use the *Questions for reflection* to help you if you want.
2. Read the story in your Bible. Read it slowly and carefully. Read it more than once. Listen to the words, and if a word or sentence draws your attention, hold it in your mind. Think over it silently—dwell on it until it sinks deep into your heart. Carry it with you into whatever you are doing for the rest of the day.
3. Do you know the meaning of your name or why your parents chose it? How important is your name to you?
4. Draw or paint a table set for a party. Draw or paint all the people you would invite, sitting around it. Write down why you would invite each one.
5. Write a letter from one of the poor or sick people in Jesus' story, telling the rich man how it felt to be invited to his party.

## Prayer

*Jesus, you call each one of us by our names. We are all important to you. Help us to accept your invitation and follow you willingly and gladly. Amen*

# The lost son

'There was once a man who had two sons. The younger one said to him, "Father, give me my share of the property now." So the man divided his property between his two sons. After a few days the younger son sold his part of the property and left home with the money.'

**Luke 15:11–32**

 **Key verses**: 11–13a

# Introduction

God's love for us is limitless and unconditional. He waits for us to come home to him with open arms. As she listens to Jesus telling a story, Deborah is made to think again about forgiveness and love.

# Story

Deborah pummelled the soft dough and began to knead it firmly with her knuckles. She frowned thoughtfully as she worked, her dark eyes veiled by a thick curtain of black hair that fell over her cheeks no matter how many times she raised her head and flicked it back.

'Deborah,' her mother called from the doorway, 'I'm going up to the roof now to hang out some washing. When you've finished, you can come and give me a hand.'

Her mother disappeared into the bright sunlight and Deborah carried on kneading. 'It's not fair,' she muttered. 'I've got to do everything whilst *Sarah*,' she spat the name angrily, 'sweet little sister Sarah, can go out and play.'

She flicked her hair back fiercely with a toss of her head and dug her knuckles deep into the creamy-coloured dough. Once she thought the dough was ready, she put it to one side and left it to rise. Baking the day's bread was the most important job in the house, and Deborah was proud that her mother trusted her to do it. But her sister Sarah should have been here to help—here to watch, so that one day she would be able to bake bread too.

Wiping her hands on a damp cloth, Deborah inspected the dough once more before following her mother outside. In the street, the glare from the whitewashed walls of the houses, standing shimmering in the sun, made her blink furiously.

Deborah shaded her eyes with one hand and grasped the ladder that led up to the flat roof with the other. She could hear her mother singing as she hung the clothes over the parapet around the roof to dry.

'I've left the dough to rise, Mum,' she called when she reached the top of the ladder. 'But Sarah still hasn't come back.'

Her mother looked up and smiled. 'Thank you, Deborah,' she said. 'Don't worry about Sarah, she'll come back when she's ready.'

Deborah stomped on to the roof. She grasped a handful of wet clothes and began to slap them over the low parapet that ran around the edge. 'Don't worry about Sarah,' she mimicked her mother under her breath. 'She'll come back when she's ready.'

'De-bor-ah!' A sing-song voice cut suddenly through her thoughts. 'Deborah, where are you?'

Deborah leaned over the parapet and glared down at the dainty figure of her sister, fluttering about like a sparrow in the street below. 'I'm up here,' she snarled, 'helping Mum.'

Sarah looked up, her bright eyes shining with excitement. 'Come quickly,' she called. 'Jesus is here, in the marketplace, and he's telling stories.'

Behind her, Deborah heard her mother laugh. 'Go on,' she said. 'I'll finish the washing.'

Deborah hesitated. She wanted to go and hear Jesus. She had heard so much about him. Everyone was talking of how he healed the sick and taught people about God and told wonderful stories. But she did not want to go with Sarah.

'Go on,' insisted her mother, 'before it's too late.'

By the time Deborah had scrambled down the ladder, Sarah had disappeared into the crowd of people flocking to hear Jesus. Deborah followed, pushing her way through farmers and shopkeepers, housewives and children, until she found herself in the marketplace, in front of the village well.

On the rough stone wall at the side, with his eyes shut against the strong mid-morning sun, sat Jesus. And sitting on the hard earth at Jesus' feet, her arms wrapped around her knees, her shining eyes fixed on his face, was Sarah.

'So there you are, Sarah,' Deborah snapped.

At the sound of her voice, Jesus looked up. Deborah's eyes caught his and he held out his hand, took hold of hers and pulled her to sit down in front of him as well.

Then Jesus motioned to the crowd to be quiet, settled himself comfortably on the wall and said in a strong voice that rang out over their heads, 'Here's another story about how happy God is when even one person is sorry for what they've done wrong.

'There was once a farmer who had two sons. The younger one liked to enjoy himself and was bored living on the farm. He wanted to spend money and have a good time, so one day he went to his father and said, "Can I have my share of your money now, Father? I want to leave home and do what I like. You'll still have my brother to work for you. Please let me go."

'The farmer felt sad that his son wanted to leave, but he said, "Very well, you can have your share of the money, if that's what you want."

'So the boy packed his bags and left. He went to a country far away and began to have a good time.'

At that point, Jesus paused. People were pressing forward, straining to hear, hanging on his every word. Deborah thought about the story as she waited for him to go on. So the younger son had gone to enjoy himself and the older one was left at home. That sounded familiar.

'At first,' Jesus continued, letting his gaze wander searchingly over the faces of the crowd, 'he enjoyed himself and made plenty of friends. But soon he had wasted all his money and his new friends disappeared. He hadn't even enough money left to buy food.

'So he tried to find work, but the only job he could get was on a farm looking after the pigs. As he sat at the side of the pig-sty, watching the pigs guzzling their food, he was so hungry that he almost jumped in and joined them.

'And he began to think, "How stupid I am, sitting here starving. Why did I leave my father's house? Even his servants have as much as they want to eat. I know what I'll do, I'll go home and tell my father I'm sorry. I'll say, 'I've done wrong in God's eyes and in yours. I don't deserve to be called your son. Take me on as a servant and I'll work for you.'" So he left the pigs and set off on the long journey home.'

Gradually, Jesus' voice faded away into silence and the men and women around him began to cough and stretch, as if they were waking from a dream. Deborah smiled smugly and glanced sideways at her sister, sitting fixed like a statue on the hard earth. Sarah's eyes had not moved so much as a hair's breadth from Jesus' face.

No wonder, Deborah thought. Because she knows she's like the good-for-nothing son. Deborah chuckled to herself. She couldn't wait until Jesus got to the next part of the story. The father was bound to throw that good-for-nothing out.

Suddenly, Jesus stood up. He shaded his eyes with his hand and moved his head, as if he was looking for someone. Then he said, 'The boy's father had been watching for him, hoping he might come back. When he was still a long way off, he saw him. The boy looked so poor and miserable that his father's heart went out to him. He raced down the road, flung his arms around his son and kissed him.'

Now Jesus opened his own arms wide, then clasped them across his chest, as if he was hugging the boy to himself. Smiling, his eyes full of radiant love, Jesus began to speak again. 'The boy was amazed by his father's welcome, and started to say he was sorry. He said, "Father, I've done wrong in God's eyes and yours too. I don't deserve to be called your son."

'But before he could say any more, his father called to his servants, "Bring the best clothes you can find and put them on my son. Put a ring on his finger and shoes on his feet. Then we'll have a party, a great feast to celebrate. For this son of mine I thought was dead, is alive again. He was lost, but now he has been found."'

Sitting down, Jesus put his hands on the wall at either side of him and leaned forward, staring at the ground. The crowd stood watching him, motionless and quiet. But Deborah tore her eyes away. Was that the end of the story? she asked herself angrily. That good-for-nothing, forgiven by his father after all he'd done?

Slowly, the low hum of voices spread through the crowd. People began to mutter among themselves and gaze around. Presently, Jesus looked up and smiled at the faces in front of him. In an instant, all eyes were on him as he began to speak once more.

'In the meantime, the older brother was out working in the fields. On his way back to the house he heard the sound of music and dancing. So he called one of the servants and asked him, "What's going on?"

'"Your brother's come back home," the servant said, "and your father is giving a party to celebrate."

'The oldest son was furious and refused to go into the house. So his father came out and begged him to come in. "No, I won't," he stormed. "Why are you having a party for him, after all he's done? All these years I've slaved for you while this son of yours was off enjoying himself and wasting your money. And never once, not once, did you let me have a party for my friends. It's not fair!"'

No, it's not fair, thought Deborah angrily as Jesus paused for breath. The oldest son had stayed at home, been obedient, done his duty.

'"My son," Jesus' firm voice rang out as he went on again, "you have always been with me, and everything I have is yours. But we had to celebrate and be happy today. This is your brother; it seemed as though he was dead, and now he's alive. Your brother was lost, but now he has been found."'

Deborah stared at Jesus, wondering what the oldest son was going to do next. But Jesus said nothing. He just folded his arms in front of his chest and sighed. The story was finished.

Now Jesus' words echoed searchingly inside Deborah's head. 'Celebrate and be happy. This is your brother. He has been found.' Round and round they went, swirling like blown leaves, until she shook her head in bewilderment.

Then Jesus turned and his eyes caught hers. All at once her confusion dissolved in his look of overwhelming love, as she began to understand. What was it Jesus had said at the beginning of the story? 'How happy God is when even one person is sorry for what they've done wrong.'

As Jesus shifted his gaze to the men and women around him, Deborah reached out to her sister. She grasped Sarah's hands in hers and said, 'Oh Sarah, let's celebrate and be happy too.'

For a moment, Sarah looked puzzled, then she smiled at Deborah and nodded her head. 'But first I'm going home to help Mum. And then you can teach me how to bake bread.'

Deborah squeezed her hands and pulled her sister to her feet. 'Come on, then,' she said. 'We'll both go home and help. And we can celebrate later, when we've finished, together.'

Now close your eyes and imagine the world of the story as if you were there. Become part of it. You can be someone in the crowd, one of the sisters, or anyone in the story you want to be. Picture yourself there, then move through the story in your imagination as the person you have chosen to be. Or, if you prefer, you can imagine you are trying to describe what is happening to someone else.

✣

Now, close your eyes, sit up straight and put your hands on your knees. Keep your body still, as this helps your mind to be still and concentrate as you go on your prayer journey. Take a deep breath and relax. Sit still and quiet and spend a few moments being with God, saying slowly and silently in your mind, '*Be still and know that I am God.*'

✣

Picture Deborah making the bread. See her flick her hair back and dig her knuckles deep into the creamy-coloured dough. Think how she is feeling...

Picture the street of houses as she goes outside. Watch her climb up to the roof and help her mother hang the clothes out to dry... Listen to Sarah calling to Deborah. See Deborah lean over the parapet and glare down at her. Hear what their mother says...

Follow Deborah through the crowd. Picture Jesus sitting on the wall at the side of the well. Watch as he pulls Deborah to sit down next to Sarah...

Listen to Jesus telling the story. Imagine the son asking for money. Picture the father as his son leaves home. Think how the father is feeling... Watch the boy as he wastes his money enjoying himself with his new friends... See him sitting at the side of the pig-sty. Smell the pigs. Feel how miserable he is... Hear Jesus' voice fade into silence as he says, 'So he left the pigs and set off on the long journey home.' ...

Watch Deborah smile smugly at Sarah. Think about how she is feeling. Wonder what Sarah is feeling...

See Jesus stand up, open his arms wide, then clasp them across his chest. See his eyes full of radiant love... Hear him tell how the father in the story welcomed his son back. Think how the father is feeling... Picture Jesus as he sits down and stares at the ground. Notice the crowd begin to mutter and gaze around. Listen to the voices die away as he begins the next part of the story...

Imagine the older brother as he comes in from the fields. Picture him with his father. Listen to what they are saying. Think how his father is feeling. Think how he is feeling...

Watch Deborah stare at Jesus. See Jesus turn and look at her... Look at Sarah as Deborah reaches out to her. Think about how they are feeling. Listen to what they say. Watch them as they walk home together.

✣

Now sit in the silence for a few moments more and think about what God is saying to you through the story. Think about how you feel. Think about what you would like to say to God and to Jesus. Thank God for his love.

## Questions for reflection

❂ Who were you in the prayer journey through the story?

❂ What was it like to hear Jesus telling a story?

- What did you think about how Deborah was feeling at the beginning of your prayer journey?
- How did you feel when you saw Deborah smile smugly at Sarah?
- Describe how you felt when you saw Jesus stand up and open his arms wide.
  Could you see the love in his eyes?
- What did you think Jesus was saying through his story?
- How did you feel when you saw Deborah stare at Jesus at the end of the story, and Jesus turn to look at her?
- What did you think when Deborah reached out to Sarah?
- How did you feel when you heard what they said to each other?
  - What do you think Jesus is saying to you? What do you want to say to him?

## Look Out

1. Use your prayer journal. Write down what you saw, heard, felt and did during your prayer journey. Use the *Questions for reflection* to help you if you want.

2. Read the story in your Bible. Read it slowly and carefully. Read it more than once. Listen to the words, and if a word or sentence draws your attention, hold it in your mind. Think over it silently—dwell on it until it sinks deep into your heart. Carry it with you into whatever you are doing for the rest of the day.

3. Our thoughts and our imaginations can make us feel happy or sad, peaceful or angry. We can learn to let bad feelings go

by using our breathing. Practise doing this. Take a deep breath. Think of breathing in God's love and, as you breathe out, let the bad feelings go—breathe them out. Or say the word 'peace', 'love' or 'Jesus' silently in your mind as you breathe in and out.

4. Plan a party for someone you love. Design invitations, decorations, a menu.

5. What is your favourite colour? Colours can affect our feelings. Use powder paint to mix as many different colours as you can. Paint a happy picture, a sad picture, an angry picture, a peaceful picture. Which colours did you use?

## Prayer

Dear God, I praise you and thank you for your limitless and unconditional love. Give me an open and generous heart, that I may be willing to forgive and willing to see myself and others in the light of your love.

# The little tax collector

Jesus went on into Jericho and was passing through. There was a chief tax collector there named Zacchaeus, who was rich. He was trying to see who Jesus was, but he was a little man and could not see Jesus because of the crowd. So he ran ahead of the crowd and climbed a sycamore tree to see Jesus, who was going to pass that way.

**Luke 19:1–9**

 **Key verses**: 1–4

# Introduction

Zacchaeus was determined to see Jesus. He was hated and despised by everyone, but was reaching out for God's love. Joshua, his servant boy, needed that love too.

# Story

The beggar squatting outside the gates stretched out his hand and tugged at the hem of Joshua's tunic as he hurried by. 'Spare a coin for an old man, young master?'

Joshua glanced down, horrified to see that the hand was filthy and covered in sores. 'How dare you touch me?' he said, pulling away. 'Go and grovel in the dirt somewhere else. This is Zacchaeus' house and he's got no time for beggars.'

The beggar spat noisily on the ground. 'Zacchaeus, eh? I've heard of him. He's one of the chief tax collectors for the thieving Romans. Cheats and steals, just like they do.'

'Get out of my way!' shouted Joshua. 'And if I see you begging around here again, you'll be sorry.'

Turning on his heel, Joshua strode through the iron gates and into the courtyard of one of the most sumptuous villas in the whole of Jericho. Once inside, he stopped for a moment to watch a small boy who was busily brushing the garden steps.

'Not like that, you little idiot,' he called. Joshua marched up to the boy and wrenched the brush from his dirty hands with a snarl.

'You need water, Nathan, water,' said Joshua, prodding the terrified boy with the end of the brush. 'The dust's going everywhere. Get some water and clean the steps properly.'

'Yes, Joshua,' whimpered Nathan, 'I'll do it now. Straight away.'

Joshua smiled and threw the brush on the ground. 'Good,' he said. 'You know how proud the master is of his Roman villa.'

'Joshua!' The sound of Zacchaeus' high, irritated voice calling his name made Joshua's mouth tighten into a thin grey line. 'See that you do it properly!' he shot at Nathan, before turning and running back across the courtyard.

'Joshua, where are you, boy?' the voice called again as he reached the villa's heavy open door and disappeared inside.

A small man standing in the shady inner courtyard beckoned Joshua impatiently with a wave of his hand. Swivelling round, Zacchaeus swept through a high archway and into a spacious room, where he sat down on some cushions at the side of a long, low table. Joshua followed.

'You've taken your time,' complained Zacchaeus.

'I'm sorry, sir,' said Joshua. 'I stopped to...'

'I'm sorry, sir,' repeated Zacchaeus. 'How many times have I heard that?' He banged his fist down hard on the table. 'Well, sorry's not good enough. If you can't do as you're told, when you're told, I'll just have to get rid of you and find someone else who can.'

Hanging his head, Joshua hoped desperately that his master could not see the red glow burning his cheeks, and that the hot tears stinging under his eyelids would not fall. Joshua had no home but this, and if Zacchaeus threw him out he would have nowhere to go.

'So, is everything ready?' demanded Zacchaeus. 'All those pilgrims passing through to Jerusalem—must make sure they pay their taxes.' He grinned and let out a high-pitched laugh. 'It's going to be an expensive day for some of them.'

Joshua raised his head and nodded. 'The toll booths are open. Some of the tax collectors have arrived already.'

'And so they should,' said Zacchaeus. 'Chief tax collectors can afford to be a little late.' He stood up and pulled his rich robes around him like a shield. 'Pick up my accounts and let's go.'

In the courtyard, Nathan was mumbling to himself as he washed down the steps. But this time Joshua hurried past, ignoring him in his effort to keep up with Zacchaeus. The little man was thin and wiry and could easily outrun men half his age.

Now walking, now running behind his master, it was not long before Joshua saw the bustling Jericho market square ahead of them, already full of shopkeepers and housewives, and pilgrims on their way to Jerusalem.

'Get those men in line!' shouted Zacchaeus, marching up to the tax collectors sitting at their tables in the midst of a disorderly crowd. 'Make them wait quietly.'

He strode up and down behind the tax collectors, checking their accounts, reading out lists of names and muttering under his breath. Finally he turned to Joshua. 'Pull out that chair for me to sit down, and set out my accounts. And be quick about it, I haven't got all day.'

When everything was ready, Zacchaeus sat down and, as Joshua watched, he began to deal with the people who were now waiting quietly in line. 'Name? Address? Occupation?' Joshua heard him demand. 'Goods or money?'

There were taxes on just about everything, Joshua knew. Often the taxes were paid in goods, not money. If a man owned sheep he might pay in wool, or if he grew vines he might pay in wine. Of course, nobody wanted to pay. So they lied and made excuses, but Zacchaeus always seemed to catch them out. Everyone hated him. 'Snake, rat, dog,' they would sneer at him contemptuously under their breaths.

It was just before midday when a crowd began forming at the edge of the square. Zacchaeus looked up from his accounts, stared at the crowd and then stood up.

'Need to stretch my legs, boy,' he said. 'I think I'll take a stroll and see what's happening down there.'

Joshua followed Zacchaeus to the edge of the crowd, but they could see nothing above a mountain of heads and shoulders. Then from somewhere in front came an excited cry.

'It's him! It's Jesus! He's coming this way.' And suddenly the crowd surged forward down the street.

'Bother!' exploded Zacchaeus, turning to Joshua. 'I'll never see over this crowd. But I must see Jesus. I must see him.' He looked around frantically and began to flap up and down like a little bird.

Joshua stared at his master in astonishment. He had never seen Zacchaeus behave like this before. He'd heard of Jesus, of course. Who in all of Jericho hadn't heard of the healing and the miracles? But Joshua knew that what had amazed Zacchaeus the most was that Jesus made friends with tax collectors, and had chosen one of them as his disciple. Joshua laughed to himself. Maybe Zacchaeus wanted to be one of Jesus' disciples too.

For a moment he watched his master, and then pointed to the other side of the street. 'Master, over there,' he said. 'That alleyway's a short cut. If we're quick we can get in front of the crowd and see Jesus as he passes by.'

Zacchaeus shot like an arrow down the narrow back street, with Joshua panting behind him. At last they came out into the main street and the breathless little man stopped. They were well ahead of the crowd now, but after a while, Zacchaeus began to look up and down.

'It's no good waiting here,' he said desperately, 'I want to see him, really see him.'

Then his face brightened, and with a loud, 'Come on!' he dashed across to a large sycamore fig tree growing at the side of the road. 'Right,' he said, grinning, 'help me up.'

'H-h-help you up?' gasped Joshua.

'Please, Joshua,' said Zacchaeus. He was almost pleading now. He looked at Joshua and his eyes shone in a way that the boy had never seen before.

'Catch hold of those low branches,' Joshua told him quickly. 'Pull yourself up and I'll push you from below.'

Zacchaeus hoisted himself through the spreading branches. Then he climbed out on to a broad branch that stretched across the street. The crowd moved slowly towards them. Joshua could just pick out the figure of a tall man who seemed to be walking a few steps ahead of the rest. Was this man Jesus, he wondered? He glanced up and saw Zacchaeus' eyes peering down anxiously through the dark green leaves.

The crowd came nearer and nearer, and now it was easy to tell that the tall man must be Jesus. There was something about the way he walked, calm and unhurried, about the way he turned deliberately and thoughtfully to those who called out his name.

At last the crowd was upon them and, to Joshua's surprise, just as he reached the tree Jesus stopped. Then he threw back his head, looked up into the branches and with a voice full of laughter called out, 'Come down, Zacchaeus! I must stay at your house today.'

The crowd froze in an icy silence as the little man scrambled down the tree, stood in front of Jesus, and gazed at him with a look of astonishment and delight. But the people all around them stared at Zacchaeus stony-faced and began to grumble as the tax collector led Jesus away.

Joshua followed his master and Jesus back to the villa, just ahead of the indignant crowd. He could hear people protesting loudly to each other as they walked. 'Zacchaeus is a cheat and a liar.'

'He's nothing but a traitor and a crook.'

'What on earth is Jesus doing, choosing to go with a man like that?'

They had reached the iron gates and, as Zacchaeus swung them open, he turned round and fixed his gaze on their hostile faces. 'Listen, sir,' he said to Jesus. 'I will give half my belongings to the poor. And if I have cheated anyone, I will pay them back four times as much.'

Jesus smiled and nodded. 'Well done. You've been forgiven, Zacchaeus,' he told him, laying a hand firmly on his arm.

Inside the house the servants prepared a feast for Jesus and his disciples. As they ate and drank and laughed and talked, Joshua watched silently from the doorway. Zacchaeus seemed to have forgotten all about him. No angry shouts of 'Where's that boy?' rang out across the room.

Indeed, Zacchaeus seemed to have forgotten about everyone, except for Jesus. The little man could not do enough for him. His dark face was flooded with light as he gazed into Jesus' eyes and listened to his calm, steady voice.

Joshua sneered to himself, his heart crowded with anger and resentment as he watched them. So Zacchaeus was going to give half his belongings to the poor. He'd believe that when he saw it. Suddenly a small boy ran across the room and smiled hesitantly up at him. It was Nathan.

'Zacchaeus wants you, Joshua,' he said.

Reluctantly, Joshua went to stand in front of his master, and was amazed to hear him say, 'This is Joshua, sir, a valuable and trusted servant.'

Joshua looked at Jesus and Jesus looked back at him, steadily and lovingly, as if Joshua was the most important person in the whole world. His eyes searched Joshua's intently, reading what was in his thoughts, and suddenly Joshua knew why Zacchaeus had wanted to see Jesus. Jesus could change your life, if you let him look into your heart.

Then Zacchaeus said, 'I'm going to start here and now. Take this money, Joshua, and give it to any beggars sitting outside my gate.'

The beggar squatting outside flinched and lifted his arm as Joshua walked through the iron gates and into the street. 'Don't be scared, old man,' he said, thrusting some coins into the old man's hand. 'This is Zacchaeus' house, and we've always got time for beggars.'

## Look in

In a moment, you are going to close your eyes and imagine the world of the story as if you were there. Become part of it. You can be yourself, Joshua, Zacchaeus, or anyone in the story you want to be. Picture yourself there, then move through the story in your imagination as the person you have chosen to be. Or, if you prefer, you can imagine you are trying to describe what is happening to someone else.

❖

Now, close your eyes, sit up straight and put your hands on your knees. Keep your body still, as this helps your mind to be still and concentrate as you go on your prayer journey. Take a deep breath and relax. Sit still and quiet and spend a few moments being with God, saying slowly and silently in your mind, *'Be still and know that I am God.'*

❖

Imagine the beggar outside Zacchaeus' beautiful house. It's a hot morning. Picture the iron gates and the high stone walls surrounding the house, keeping people out… Watch Joshua as the beggar touches him. Listen to what Joshua says. Think how the beggar feels…

See Joshua go into the courtyard. Notice Nathan brushing the steps. Watch what Joshua does to him. Listen to what he says…

Hear Zacchaeus shout 'Joshua!' Picture Joshua following Zacchaeus into the spacious room. Listen to what Zacchaeus says to him. Think how Joshua is feeling…

Follow Zacchaeus and Joshua as they go to the market square. See the tax collectors sitting at their tables. Listen to Zacchaeus when he marches up and down behind them... Look at Zacchaeus sitting at his table. Hear him demanding people's names, addresses, occupations. Think how the people feel...

Imagine the crowd at the edge of the square. Watch Zacchaeus and Joshua trying to look over their heads. See the crowd surge forward... Look at Zacchaeus as he flaps up and down. Hear him mutter, 'Must see Jesus.' Notice Joshua staring in astonishment...

Follow them as they run up the alleyway. See Zacchaeus dash to the tree. Picture Joshua helping Zacchaeus climb into the branches. Wonder what Joshua is thinking. Wonder what Zacchaeus is thinking... Notice the crowd move towards them. Watch Jesus turn to the people who call out his name...

Picture Jesus as he stops under the tree. See him look up into the branches and call out, 'Come down, Zacchaeus! I must stay at your house today.' ... Watch Zacchaeus scramble down from the tree. Look at him standing in front of Jesus. Think how he feels...

Listen to what the people are saying. Think how they feel. Hear Zacchaeus say to Jesus, 'I will give half my belongings to the poor.' Think about how Jesus feels...

Imagine the feast in Zacchaeus' house. Picture Joshua standing at the door watching... Follow Joshua as he goes to Zacchaeus. Watch him look at Jesus. Watch Jesus look at him. Think how Joshua feels...

Hear Zacchaeus say, 'Take this money, Joshua.' Picture Joshua giving the beggar the money. Wonder what the beggar is thinking.

❖

Now sit in the silence for a few moments more and think about what God is saying to you through the story. Think about how you feel. Think about what you would like to say to God and to Jesus. Thank God for his love.

## Questions for reflection

- Who were you in the prayer journey through the story?
- What did you think when you heard Joshua talking to the beggar and Nathan at the beginning of your prayer journey?
- What did you think when you heard Zacchaeus talking to Joshua?
- How did you feel when you heard Zacchaeus asking people their names and addresses?
- What did you think when you heard Zacchaeus say, 'I must see Jesus' and saw him climb into the tree?
- What did you think when Jesus called, 'Come down, Zacchaeus! I must stay at your house today'?
- How did you feel when you heard Zacchaeus say to Jesus, 'I will give half my belongings to the poor'?
- What was it like to watch Joshua and Jesus looking at each other?
- How did you feel when you saw Joshua give the beggar some money?
  - What do you think Jesus is saying to you? What do you want to say to him?

## Look out

1. Use your prayer journal. Write down what you saw, heard, felt and did during your prayer journey. Use the *Questions for reflection* to help you if you want.

112

2. Read the story in your Bible. Read it slowly and carefully. Read it more than once. Listen to the words, and if a word or sentence draws your attention, hold it in your mind. Think over it silently—dwell on it until it sinks deep into your heart. Carry it with you into whatever you are doing for the rest of the day.

3. Who has helped you to grow into the person you are now? Write the story of your life so far, saying who has helped and encouraged you along the way, and how.

4. Draw a comic-strip version of Zacchaeus' meeting with Jesus.

5. Sow some cress seeds in two trays. Put one tray in the sunlight and water it. Put the other in the dark. Watch what happens to plants if they are not cared for. The same thing can happen to our spirits.

## Prayer

Dear God, we know that you loved us so much that you sent Jesus to show us the way back to you. Help us to say 'yes' when you call us, to do willingly what you ask us to do, and to grow daily in our love of you. Amen

# Five loaves and two fishes

After this, Jesus went across Lake Galilee (or, Lake Tiberias, as it is also called). A large crowd followed him, because they had seen his miracles of healing those who were ill. Jesus went up a hill and sat down with his disciples.

**John 6:1–15**

 **Key verses: 1–3**

# Introduction

Benjamin had five loaves and two fishes. Not enough food to feed 5000 people. But Jesus took it and worked a miracle. We may think we have little to give to Jesus, but he needs our help. If we put ourselves into his hands, we will be amazed to discover what he can do with us and through us.

# Story

Benjamin scooped up a handful of stones, hurled them into the lake and scowled as they disappeared beneath the calm blue water. He squinted into the distance, watching the ripples radiating outwards, and pictured the fury in his father's face when he had dragged Benjamin out of the synagogue yesterday.

'I've just about had enough of you, sitting in the synagogue reading every day while your brothers do all the work!' his father had exploded at him.

'But Joshua,' his mother had sighed, 'you know he wants to be a teacher.'

'A teacher?' his father had exploded again. 'Rubbish! All that book-learning. What good would it do him?' His father had wagged an impatient finger. 'Listen to me, Benjamin. You'd better get yourself out into the fields right now and help your brothers. And if I catch you sitting reading in that synagogue again, God help you.'

As he remembered his father's angry words, Benjamin's eyes filled with tears. The thing he wanted most of all in the world was to be a teacher, not a farmer. Teachers didn't work in the fields.

And so Benjamin had run away. He was going to Jerusalem, to the temple, to learn to be a teacher there. But it was a long way to Jerusalem and he had only walked a few dusty miles since first light, skirting the sheep-dotted fields and thick olive groves, clambering over the rocks and pebbles to the shores of Lake Galilee below.

Yawning, Benjamin stretched his arms, then sat down and leaned back against a smooth rock. He closed his eyes to shut out the glare of the hot, high sun, and dozed restlessly in the silence, until the sound of voices coming over the hill brought him jumping to his feet.

Three men appeared, gabbling loudly to each other and pointing into the distance. As they approached Benjamin, they called out.

'Have you seen him? Did he pass this way?'

'Who are you looking for?' Benjamin asked.

'Jesus, of course. Jesus of Nazareth, the teacher.'

Without waiting for his reply, they stumbled on. Benjamin shrugged and picked up the basket of food he had hurriedly packed for the journey. 'Jesus of Nazareth?' he shouted after them. 'Never heard of him.'

He dusted himself down and was just about to find the path again when a woman appeared with a baby on her hip and a small boy pulling at her skirts. Following the woman came a shopkeeper Benjamin knew, and two farmers. Slowly, a long stream of people poured after them over the hill. Beggars dressed in rags, blind people, friends carrying the sick, first a trickle and then wave upon wave of them, swept onwards like the relentless waters of Lake Galilee itself.

Benjamin scratched his head. Were they all looking for this teacher, this person called Jesus of Nazareth? he wondered. There must be thousands of them. Try as he might to pass through the other way, he was soon caught up in the flood of people that flowed over the rocks and on to the grassy slopes. The crowd pressed in on him from either side, and the smells of dank sweat and sour breath choked the air around him.

'Must find Jesus, even if it takes all day,' they called to each other.

'Did you see him when he made that lame boy walk?'

'Did you see the blind woman when he healed her eyes?'

'Did you hear the wonderful stories he told?'

Benjamin thought they must all be crazy. A lame boy walking and a blind woman seeing? He decided to get away from them as fast as he could. Elbowing forward, he struggled to free himself from the sea of people, but was swept along by the swell of the surging crowd until it stopped at last at the foot of a flower-dotted hill. Now he could get away. He swung round to pick out a path among the people, stumbled over a pair of feet, put out his hand to stop himself from falling and looked up.

Sitting on a rock a little way above him, surrounded by a small group of men, sat a man with his eyes closed and his upturned face lit by the clear light of the late morning sun. Benjamin stared at him, curious. This must be the Jesus they were all talking about.

Behind Benjamin, men and women sat down on the grass, or stood huddled together in groups. Voices hushed, and calmness cloaked the hillside like a warm coat. Only the cries of children and the sick could be heard now as the crowd waited expectantly for Jesus to speak.

Presently, Jesus opened his eyes, smiled at the men beside him and stood up. Benjamin looked at Jesus and gasped. He could see a bright, dazzling light all around him. Benjamin rubbed his eyes and looked again. He must be seeing things. But no, the light was still there. He wondered if anyone else could see it, and turned to the men behind him. But he was too afraid to ask. Supposing they thought he'd gone mad?

At last Jesus began to speak, and his voice rang out over the heads of the people, clear and powerful. After a while, Jesus began to walk up and down, talking, laughing, listening, teaching, making his way towards those who called his name as the crowd pushed and shoved to get near him.

'Jesus, over here, my wife can't walk.'

'Jesus, this way, my baby's sick.'

'Jesus, look at me, I'm going blind.'

Benjamin edged his way forward through the mass of people to follow Jesus, drawn by the light around him like a firefly to a flame. From where he stood, he stared in amazement as he saw an old woman get up from the grass and walk at the touch of Jesus' hand. He whistled in astonishment when a blind boy opened his eyes and began to see. He shook his head in wonder when Jesus took a sick child into his arms and made her well.

Incredible things were happening all around him—impossible things, but they were happening all the same. Benjamin trailed behind Jesus like a shadow all afternoon, forgetting about Jerusalem, until the hot sun sank in the sky and evening came. At last Jesus sat down and eased himself back against the rocks, his eyes shut.

But the crowds who had come to hear him would not go away. They still sat or stood there, on the trampled grass and the sharp stones, looking hungry and tired, but waiting expectantly for Jesus to begin teaching and healing again. After a time he raised himself up on his elbows and gazed at the great sea of faces.

Slowly he sat up and turned to one of his disciples. Then Benjamin heard him say, 'Philip, where can we buy enough food to feed all these hungry people?'

Philip shrugged his shoulders and shook his head. 'It would cost more than I could earn in two hundred days.'

Jesus' other disciples shook their heads as well. 'There's nowhere to buy food around here,' they said. 'Send the people away so that they can go into the villages and buy food themselves.'

'No,' insisted Jesus firmly, 'it's too far. They need some food before they go. You must give them something to eat.'

So Jesus' disciples decided to go among the people and ask if anyone had food to share. But those who had brought food had already eaten it, while most of the crowd had had nothing to eat all day. What Jesus had asked his disciples to do seemed impossible.

Benjamin heard them calling, 'Has anyone any food?' as they walked up and down.

He looked inside the basket he had taken from the house that morning. Amazed by the wonderful things he had seen Jesus doing, he had been too excited to think about eating at all. Benjamin unwrapped the cloth around his food. Inside were five small barley loaves and two small pickled fish. He stared at them. There was not much there to share with anyone, and besides, he was hungry.

Then he thought about the light around Jesus, and the old woman walking and the blind boy seeing and the sick child laughing. In a flash, he jumped to his feet and ran towards a tall fisherman whom he'd heard Jesus call Andrew.

'I've got five loaves and two fishes,' he cried excitedly and held out his basket.

The fisherman took Benjamin by the hand and led him to Jesus. 'Master,' he said, 'there is a boy here with five loaves and two fishes, but that's not enough to feed all these people.'

Benjamin smiled at Jesus. He held the basket out confidently. Jesus smiled at Benjamin and nodded.

'This is just what I needed,' he said.

Then he turned to his friends and pointed to the crowd. 'Make everyone sit down, so that it's easier to share out the food.'

Jesus took the bread out of the basket. Benjamin held his breath and wondered what he would do. Then Jesus broke it and lifted his face towards the sky. He thanked God for the food and blessed it, and then began to give out the bread and fishes to his disciples to share among the people.

Benjamin stood next to Jesus, a huge smile splitting his face from ear to ear as he watched. Jesus went on and on sharing out the food. Again and again his disciples came back to get the bread and fish and take it to the people. But the food did not come to an end. Jesus' hands were always full and he always had more to give. Benjamin whistled. Would Jesus never stop? There

must have been five thousand people there on the hillside that day, but every one of them was fed.

Finally, when the crowd had had enough, Jesus pointed to the grass and said, 'Now pick up the scraps that are left, so that nothing is wasted.'

Without hesitating, Benjamin helped Jesus' disciples to pick up the pieces. They filled twelve baskets with the scraps that were left over.

'Did you see what he did with the bread and the fish?' men and women called to each other as Benjamin ran up and down among them. 'It's amazing; it's a miracle.'

Climbing back up the hill towards Jesus, Benjamin began to feel tired. It had been the most exciting day of his life, but he still had to walk the long road to Jerusalem. At the thought of it, his heart sank. Did he really need to go all that way?

'Benjamin!' He lifted his head as a familiar voice cut through his thoughts. To his amazement he saw his father, trudging wearily over the grass towards him. Benjamin stood still, not knowing whether to run or stay. 'Saw you go off over the fields,' his father panted. 'Been trying to find you all day.'

'I'm going to Jerusalem,' Benjamin declared defiantly as his father came up close, 'to learn to be a teacher.'

His father shook his head. 'Jerusalem? You don't need to go to Jerusalem. It seems to me that there's a man,' he pointed up the hill towards Jesus, 'who can teach you all you need to know.' His father sniffed loudly. 'It seems to me I got it wrong about teachers.'

Benjamin gazed wonderingly into his father's face. 'And so did I,' he said. 'Teachers work wherever they're needed, and teach wherever they work.' He put his hand on his father's arm. 'Wait for me a minute, father,' he said.

Jesus turned as Benjamin came towards him, and Benjamin stopped to look at him, his heart pounding. The sun had almost disappeared but the light that surrounded Jesus was stronger than ever. With a welcoming smile, Jesus held out his arms and Benjamin ran, stumbling over the sharp rocks and trodden-down flowers until he fell, joyfully, into those arms.

Jesus bent his head until it touched Benjamin's. 'Thank you for your help, Benjamin,' he whispered. 'I could not have done anything without you.'

## Look in

In a moment, you are going to close your eyes and imagine the world of the story as if you were there. Become part of it. You can be yourself or Benjamin, or anyone in the story you want to be. Picture yourself there, then move through the story in your imagination as the person you have chosen to be. Or, if you prefer, you can imagine you are trying to describe what is happening to someone else.

❖

Now, close your eyes, sit up straight and put your hands on your knees. Keep your body still, as this helps your mind to be still and concentrate as you go on your prayer journey. Take a deep breath and relax. Sit still and quiet and spend a few moments being with God, saying slowly and silently in your mind, *'Be still and know that I am God.'*

❖

Imagine Benjamin standing beside the calm blue water of Lake Galilee. It's a hot day and sunlight is falling on the rocks and pebbles on the shore below... Think about how he feels as he remembers his father's angry words... Watch him sit down and fall asleep. Then see him jump up as three men appear and ask about Jesus...

Now follow Benjamin as he gets caught up in the crowd. See the beggars, the women with babies, the sick people, the blind people. Feel them pressing in on him, listen to what they are saying… Watch Benjamin as he struggles to get away. Think about how he feels. Picture him as he stumbles and looks up at Jesus…

See Jesus stand up. Look at his face. Look at the bright, dazzling light all around him. Watch Benjamin rub his eyes and look at Jesus again…

Hear Jesus' clear, powerful voice. Follow him as he walks up and down among the crowd. See him touch the old woman and make her walk. Watch the blind boy open his eyes. See him take the sick child in his arms and make her well… Picture Benjamin trailing behind Jesus. Wonder what he is thinking…

Look at Jesus as he sits down. Think about how he feels… Hear him talk to his disciples. Listen to what they say… Imagine the disciples walking among the crowd.

Watch Benjamin look in his basket and run to the fisherman… Picture him holding out his basket to Jesus. Hear Jesus say, 'This is just what I needed.' …

Watch Jesus as he breaks the bread, thanks God and blesses the food… Look at Jesus sharing out the food. See the disciples come back again and again to get the bread and the fish. Think how they feel. Look at Jesus' full hands… Picture Benjamin and the disciples picking up the scraps. Listen to what the people are saying…

Imagine Benjamin climbing back up the hill. See his father trudge towards him. Listen to what they are saying…

Watch Benjamin run to Jesus. See Jesus hold out his arms. Look at the light around him. Hear Jesus say, 'I could not have done anything without you.'

❖

Now sit in the silence for a few moments more and think about what God is saying to you through the story. Think about how you feel. Think about what you would like to say to God and to Jesus. Thank God for his love.

## Questions for reflection

- Who were you in the prayer journey through the story?
- What did you think about the things Benjamin's father said to him at the beginning of the story?
- How did you feel when you heard the people in the crowd talking about the things that Jesus had done?
- Could you see the light around Jesus? What did it look like?
- What was it like to see Jesus healing people?
- What did you think when Benjamin gave his basket of food to Jesus?
- Describe how you felt when you saw Jesus sharing out the food.
- How did you feel when you saw Benjamin run to Jesus and heard Jesus say, 'I could not have done anything without you?
- What do you think Jesus is saying to you? What do you want to say to him?

## Look out

1. Use your prayer journal. Write down what you saw, heard, felt and did during your prayer journey. Use the *Questions for reflection* to help you if you want.

2. Read the story in your Bible. Read it slowly and carefully. Read it more than once.
Listen to the words, and if a word or sentence draws your attention, hold it in your mind. Think over it silently—dwell

on it until it sinks deep into your heart. Carry it with you into whatever you are doing for the rest of the day.

3. Decorate a candle. Use sequins, glitter, sticky shapes. Make a holder from clay.

4. Love is like a magnet. When we give love, we attract love. Draw two magnets. Write the name of someone you love on the arm of one magnet. Write why you love them on the other arm. Write your name on one arm of the other magnet. Write why people love you on the other arm.

5. Think about all the hungry people in the world. How can you help them? How can we help them? How can our government help them? How can they help themselves?

## Prayer

Jesus, here I am, ready to work with you. I offer you my whole self for you to use for the good of others.

Amen

# Appendix

## A selection of children's responses following their prayer journey into the stories

I felt like Jesus was speaking to me.

I was amazed by what Jesus did.

I felt I was really there.

It was amazing to see Jesus healing all those sick and ill people.

It was very special to see Jesus healing people.

I could see the light around Jesus. It looked like the rays of the sun.

I was astounded when I saw Jesus healing people.

I could see the light around Jesus. It was very bright.

I heard Jesus' voice. I had to see him.

When I saw Jesus I felt good inside.

I just saw the story in my mind.

I could see everything as if I was there.

I heard the words that Jesus said.

I was so excited to see Jesus.

I felt that I was really the boy in the story.

It was beautiful when Jesus told a story.

I saw the whole story in my mind.

I was actually the girl in the story.

I felt loved by Jesus' eyes.

I heard Jesus say to me, 'Help others.'

It was fun to hear Jesus telling a story and it felt very special too.

Wow, I thought. Jesus asked me in his heart to join him.

Jesus smiled at me.

I could feel the peace and it was lovely. It was lovely to be silent.

I could feel the peace. It was like a breeze on a summer's day.

I could feel the peace. It was like everyone was silent in the world.

Jesus is saying, 'Be still and love.' I want to say, 'I'm still and I love.'

I didn't know that Jesus can change you.

I felt that Jesus is trying to change people's lives.

I felt that Jesus can change nearly everyone's life.

Jesus is saying, 'I can change people.'

It made me realize how easy it is to talk to God and that you can talk to him without words.

I could go right up to God and talk to him and I felt happy.

I thought how powerful Jesus is.

I felt good inside and really cheered up.

I would like to say to Jesus, 'Thank you for everything you've done for me.'

I think Jesus is saying, 'Believe in me.' I am saying, 'I do.'

I felt that Jesus was telling me to share things.

Jesus was saying to me, 'Be yourself.'

Jesus was saying, 'Come and help me.'

I want to help Jesus.

I loved Jesus.

I told Jesus he was the most important thing in my life.

Jesus is saying that everybody is worth the same to God.

Jesus is saying, 'Love God and you love everyone.'

I want to say to Jesus, 'Thank you for showing God to me.'

Jesus is saying that everyone is special whether they are rich or poor.